Myth & the Body

Stanley Keleman

Myth & the Body

A COLLOQUY WITH

Joseph Campbell

CENTER PRESS

BERKELEY, CALIFORNIA

Published by
CENTER PRESS
2045 Francisco Street
Berkeley, California 94709
WWW.CENTERPRESS.COM

ISBN 0-934320-17-9
Library of Congress Catalogue Number:
99-72350

Printed in the United States of America
3 4 5 6 7 8 9

BOOK DESIGN Burch Typografica
TEXT TYPE Sabon, designed by Jan Tschichold
DISPLAY TYPE Ružena Antikva, designed by Rodrigo Cavazos
upon the base of Vojtěch Preissig's type Preissigova

TO
JOSEPH CAMPBELL
1904-1987
friend and colleague

℘

ACKNOWLEDGEMENTS

*I am indebted to the following people
who made this book possible:
State Senator John Vasconcellos for introducing me to
the oral history program at University of California, Santa Barbara.
To David Russell of the oral history program,
UCSB, who archived and transcribed the tapes.
To Professor Richard Wiseman of San Francisco State University,
who saw the possibilities of the transcripts and
organized the first draft.*

*I am thankful to the efforts of two fine editors,
Barbara Brauer and Irene Elmer,
who read the manuscript and made suggestions.
To Jean Erdman and the Joseph Campbell Foundation for their kind
permission and enthusiasm for this project.*

*To my wife, Gail, for her unflagging support
in helping me at every stage.*

*To Terry MacClure, who was the editor and art director
of the final version of the book.*

MYTHS SERVE a practical function. They enable people to organize the experience of their own bodies. Myths dramatize the experience of our embodiment and which voice is speaking loudest at a particular time.

Our body structure determines a mythic way of thinking and gives us an identity.

STANLEY KELEMAN

We are asked, "Where do these myths come from?" On the desert, the mesomorphic type prevails. The biological ground of the myths of the desert comes from a mesomorphic biology. In the river valleys, the endomorphic type is dominant. I thought of the mesomorphic protecting god, Apollo; and the endomorphic god of the vine and nature powers, Dionysus. But what about the ectomorph? We come to Orpheus. When he was torn apart and his head torn off, his head continued to sing. The transformation of the biological into the spiritual comes right there, and we can start now to reclassify all the myths.

Instead of talking about matriarch, talk about endomorphic myths. And instead of patriarch, talk about mesomorphic. I think one can generalize and bring the myths of the world into these categories and see how they talk to our different biological needs. Now and then a real idea comes through, and this is a real one for me.

Joseph Campbell

*Myths are collective dreams, and are not to be taken as literal.
They are metaphors.*

Joseph Campbell

MYTHS ARE ABOUT the body itself. Metaphor is bodily based. It is experiential. In myth, I look for the body – its shapes, expressions, and emotional gestures. The body's growth, its deepening range of feeling and action, is what myth promises.

STANLEY KELEMAN

Table of Contents

Preface

THIS BOOK CAME TO BE with the transcription of fourteen years of taped seminars between Stanley Keleman and his good friend, mythologist Joseph Campbell.

The sheer volume of taped dialog was immense with many subjects covered. Editors were reluctant to leave anything out. Yet when Campbell and Keleman talked year after year about one particular subject – Parsifal and the Holy Grail – everything they stood for was present: Keleman for the experience of the body; Campbell for symbol and meaning.

What is new in this book is Keleman's view of Parsifal: how the changing body of Parsifal himself is instructive to our modern life. There is no interpretation, only the path of growth the body will take. The dream of a culture, myth, is no different than a personal dream. As a therapist, Keleman looks for a client's body in a dream – how they use themselves, how they move and respond, and how this may serve to instruct their daily life. And so he looks at the body of Parsifal in the myth of the Holy Grail.

TERRENCE MACCLURE
editor

Introduction

FRIENDS had arranged a meeting with Joseph Campbell. We met on a misty afternoon, on a pier in Santa Cruz, California. A handsome, athletic, older man, vital and self-possessed, approached me. I recall how firm his hand was and the friendly stance. We were to talk that day about the possibility of doing a seminar about myth and the body. This turned out to be the first of our many dialogues.

Joseph Campbell and I held annual seminars on this theme for fourteen years. And he made a statement then that still stands as the glue of our relationship and the foundation for this book: "Mythology is a song. It is the song of the imagination, inspired by the energies of the body."

For me, mythology is the poetics of the body singing about our cellular truth. Myth is a poem of the experience of being embodied and of our somatic journey. It is the song of creation, the genetic experience that has organized a way to sing, to dance, to paint, to tell stories that transmit that experience to others.

In this venture, Joseph Campbell and I were brothers; the chemistry between us was immediate. I was the practical idealist; he was the idealistic troubadour. My somatic-emotional method grounded his literary knowledge and imagination in the body. His understanding of the ancestors' visions transformed, for me, the somatic perspective and deepened my understanding of our internal, somatic reality.

Joseph Campbell knew that experience was knowledge, and that academic knowing was not the experience people were looking for. I know that experience is a bodied event, and that myth, as an organizing process, is one way to help make order from somatic experience.

The use of the Bodying Practice – in which people intensify and then disorganize their emotional postures, generating feelings and eliciting memories – intrigued him. These exercises bring the unknown body to the surface, as images, dreams, and emotional expression. They bring a vitality to the body's sense of self. The exercises evoke an inner protoplasmic stream that reminded him of Hesse's Siddartha, the ferryman sitting by the river, learning from his own inner river.

I have condensed the seminar work of many years into short essays, lifted from our dialogues. There are five parts beginning with the initial definition of body as myth, describing the hero's journey as a means of understanding our own somatic destiny, and finally, showing how we can experience a somatic, mythic reality.

$$\sim$$

PART ONE establishes the view that myths describe the experiences of the body. They are, in fact, metaphors for internal body states, experiences, and development. Myths also help the body to organize and incorporate experience.

Myths today are no longer grounded in bodily experience. We prize the body's images and symbols, its cerebral functions. This has led us to a modern Wasteland. We have forsaken the body as a source of knowledge.

PART TWO explores the body as process, and the source of somatic images and stories. Although myth speaks about the body and its inner responses, in practice this is no longer true for most of us. More and more we embody and incorporate external images that have no inner resonance. In our effort to accept the roles that society imposes, we live a life of images, ungrounded in our nature. The Bodying Practice is designed to restimulate the body's own images.

PART THREE considers our embodiment as a hero's journey – a journey that is essential to our somatic nature, deepening it and giving it individuality.

In the medieval legend of *Parsifal*, narrated by Joseph Campbell, the journey takes the form of a young, unformed adolescent traveling away from home, exposed to society's rules. His journey is to redeem his essential compassionate nature.

PART FOUR considers another stage of the hero's journey – what it means to be a mature adult. We begin to recognize that the stories we tell, our life stories, are about our bodying. Telling our stories communicates to others how to body their own experiences and how to work with their experiences to make a life.

PART FIVE explores the ways in which we can live a somatic, mythic life. We can learn to live from the body, and to form its responses for our life. Living a somatic life is living a mythic story.

JOSEPH CAMPBELL'S HERO follows a literary archetypal path:

Everyone is a hero.
This is a given.

We have a call to adventure.

We refuse.

A crisis ensues.
We cannot turn back – and we answer the call.

We collect helpers, teachers, guides.

And we cross a threshold into the unknown.

We lose our identity and enter an abyss, a nadir,
the belly of the whale.

We emerge.

We begin traveling back home to what we have known –
recrossing the threshold.

We return.

We have changed.

Myth & the Body

THIS BOOK
*describes how the
soma illuminates the mythic story
present in everyday life.*

READERS
*may find it useful to read through
the entire book first, as if listening to a talk.
Then the book can be reread as a
work method and a
conceptual
guide.*

LASCAUX TEMPLE CAVES
Jean Vertut, Issy-Les-Moulineaux

PART ONE

Body & Myth

I am embodied; therefore I experience that I am.

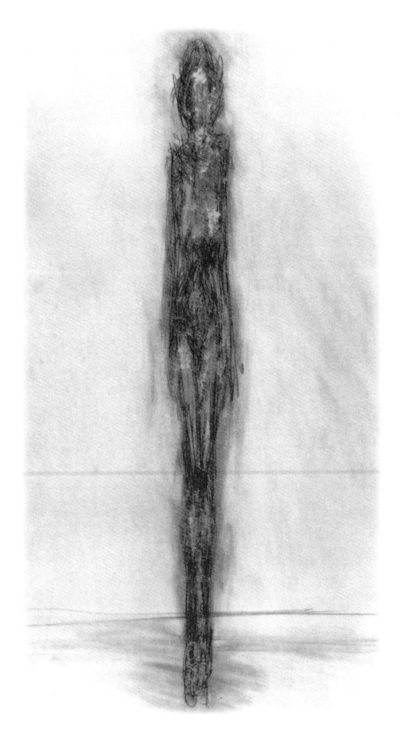

ALBERTO GIACOMETTI, "DETAIL OF STANDING WOMAN," 1946

CHAPTER I

Myth as Body

FOR ME, mythology is a function of biology . . . a product of the soma's imagination. What do our bodies say? And what are our bodies telling us? The human imagination is grounded in the energies of the body. And the organs of the body are the determinants of these energies and the conflicts between the impulse systems of the organs and the harmonization of them. These are the matters of myth.

Joseph Campbell

THE BODY is given. Myth is also given from the body.

STANLEY KELEMAN

Mythic images are anatomy

A mythic image is the shape of anatomy speaking about itself. The serpent of mythology is the spinal cord, with the beak of the pons as its head. The cortex is the thousand-petaled lotus, the crown of thorns. This makes mythic image incapable of being a reality apart from somatic reality. Mythic image is the body speaking to itself about itself. Myths are scripts of our genetic shapes in social language. They are patterns of embodiment: they show us how to grow our inherited biological endowment into a personal form.

Body and myths

Humans have always been concerned with the magical and the mythical, not only to organize a sense of place, continuity, and identity, but also to organize a way to act, to behave. In this spirit, people have always told stories about heroes and situations, cosmologies and sagas. These stories have done more than give order to existence, a way to manage the unknown. They have acted as models for the shaping of the self, the possibilities of how we form our somatic selves from the inside out. Embedded in these stories have been descriptions of the different subjective states of the body self.

When we become intimate with these stories and the models they offer, we learn the subjective narrative of our own body's multiple shapes. Myth evokes our deepest, inmost somatic self, a somatic structure with many layers of shapes that give our body depth and dimension.

Direct experience

Some people are confused because they know things without being able to say how they know them. People call it intuition. Some people are afraid to say they know with their body feeling. To know from inside our body is to be awakened by a wave of excitement. The body and its responses are a source of knowing.

Identity

I don't say, "I think, therefore I am." Rather, I say, "I am embodied; therefore I experience that I am." It is the experiencing of our embodiment that gives us the experience of being alive. It gives us our perception of a bodied past, an historical life, and it gives us a present. Each and every one of us shares in the process of embodiment.

Our perception of our own growth, subjectively as a bodily process, closely parallels the dream and poetic states that form myths. The body's brain creates linear time, and it objectifies events. In other words, mythic reality is a motile organization, like a beating heart, with tidal feelings and shapes.

Our body's story

What is a myth? A story that grows out of the history of bodily process to orient life and give values. On one level, a myth expresses a view of the social and personal world; it represents a cosmology. On another level, it tells about the trials and tribulations in the initiation into different stages of adult life. A myth is a social order that tells about familial roles, about conflict and resolution. And lastly, a myth is a delight by which to relate the many characters in the body. A myth helps to make order of life experiences, such as loyalty, sexuality, death.

Myth is a story in a particular language that humans have devised for themselves. In relating a myth, one part of the organism can talk to another, and individuals can share their internal experiences with those around them. Myth is a way of perceiving inner and outer worlds. The body organizes sensation that arise out of tissue metabolism, and this is what we call consciousness. This somatic process is the matrix for the stories and images of myth.

Experience and language

The source of myth and body knowledge is in ourselves. It is intensified by somatic interactions and conversations. If somatic experience and language are separate, we try to make sense out of our life experience by means of symbols. But when we reflect on our experience, we find that the symbols don't quite make sense. We have to re-experience the somatic aspects of our own body's symbol making.

Myth organizes a path

We can think of ourselves as a living process, continually organizing and embodying what we encounter. This is why journeys and paths are so prominent in myth. The journey is leaving the womb, leaving four-footedness and learning to stand erect. It is being young and following our path to maturity. We are on the path of our life, seeking the Grail, forming the internalized image of our promised inherited somatic self.

The effect of a myth

One way to make sense of our experience is to examine myths. Myths are easily interpreted and misinterpreted; but most importantly, they affect the roles that we take on or want to take on by ordering the way we use ourselves. How do we think about ourselves, and how do we try to enact ourselves? How do we use our brain; how do we use our pelvis; how do we use our arms? In short, how do we use ourselves to enact the known or unknown mythic images that are part of our life? Because, whether we know it or not, we are living these inherited stories.

How do we live our lives?

When we try to experience how we were born, how we formed our feelings for the connection with our beginning – and, conversely, how we form the approach to our body's end – we run into the problem of the void. What happens? We don't know. All of a sudden we become conscious, or we lose consciousness. It's a mystery. So how we begin and how we end are the two major themes of all myths.

In myth, what we see is an organism that can speak through its own layers about its past situation. To understand myth is to be intimate with how we experience our existence. The layers in myth – say in Goethe's *Faust* or in the Bible – are about bodied life during its different phases of formation. Our bodies, our somatic and emotional processes, have a beginning, a middle ground, and an end, that give our structure and imaginative functions a coherency.

Mythology is structured in the cells. Each sperm cell, each egg, contains a story that is recreated in the full growth of each cell. This is part of our history. Myth is about the body's journey, recreating itself endlessly in a particular way, to form an individual personal structure called self.

Direct expression of your experience

Myth is storytelling, a direct expression of our experiences, whether we are aware of it or not. The story that we tell ourselves is, in fact, the story of our own process. This process is the essential ingredient of our subjective self. Myth tells us about the nature of our soma's experience. Do we need a story to tell us about what is sacred? Or do we already have the experience that matches the story? Does the story evoke the experience that permits us both to sense and to make sense out of what is happening? The function of myth is to put experience into stories, because stories are the organizers of bodily experience, of ways to form ourselves as individuals.

Myth communicates our somatic humanity

We recognize myth in another way – through the immediacy of experience, which transcends social reality. The immediacy of hunger, of erection, of menstruation. The immediacy of the beating of the heart. The mythic sense is organized by what goes on inside oneself. The ability to speak about these primary experiences, to make stories about them, gives a voice to our internal reality. As human beings, we dramatize our inner experiences as somatic images. We sustain our experiences when we embody them.

endomorph

ectomorph

mesomorph

CHAPTER 2

Body as Inheritance

WE ARE PART of a biological life. At conception we receive an inherited constitution, as visceral endomorphs, muscular mesomorphs, sensory ectomorphs. Our body shape is a powerful emotional symbol of our self; it is like a mythic image that helps us to understand our roles and the multiplicity of ways we identify with those roles.

STANLEY KELEMAN

> *The ectomorphic mode is based on the individual. That might help to explain why it is a myth with no biological grounding, the rare and modern times of the ectomorphic era.*
>
> *Joseph Campbell*

ᘐᘗ

The mythic types

William Sheldon, in his theory of constitutional types, describes three temperaments based on the three embryological layers of the body.*

In the endomorphic, metabolic type, the hormones and tissues of digestion and respiration predominate. This temperament is oriented toward nurturing and intimacy.

---

* William H. Sheldon, *Atlas of Men,* Hafner Publishing Co., 1970.

In the ectomorphic type, the neural hormones and organs of sensation predominate. This temperament is oriented toward collecting sensory information.

In the mesomorphic type, hormones of action, large muscles, and bones predominate. This temperament is oriented toward action.

The endomorph arises from the visceral layer, the mesomorph from the middle layer, and the ectomorph from the outer membrane of the embryo. These somatic organizations are inherited; they determine the way in which people

experience themselves and make sense of their world. Each one is linked to a different set of myths. The mesomorph is linked to the myths of the warrior; the endomorph to the myths of the founders of agricultural communities; and the ectomorph to the myths of scholars and ascetics.

A combination of myths

We can make connections between some of the myths and William Sheldon's constitutional types. Each of us is a combination of all three. Each of us combines endo softness, meso firmness, and ecto fragility. Each of us moves toward people, against people, and away from people; or seeks power, uses power, avoids power. The degree to which we do each of these things determines the intensity and duration of our contact with the world, and the predominance of a particular inherited type.

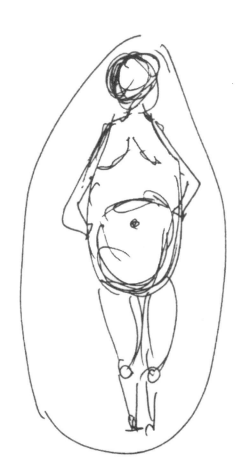

One part of our life is led by the mesomorph, the warrior adventurer, another by the intuitive, poetic endomorph.

Our body is our destiny

Our body is a process. Its structure has a way of thinking, feeling, perceiving, and organizing its experiences, an innate way of forming its responses. Since we are embodied creatures, you could say that our body is our destiny. You can revolt against your destiny; or you can try to understand it and live it in a meaningful way. Or you can seek to influence your destiny.

Who you were meant to be

Who you are supposed to be – that is, who you are asked to be by virtue of your role in a given society – may be a lot different from who you were meant to be. Who you were meant to be was determined at the moment of conception by the way your inherited body code organized your constitutional body type. Our somatic process has a big say in how we experience our sense of self and the myths and stories we identify with.

Were you born with strong bones and muscles; a powerful sympathetic nervous system, cerebellum, and thalamus; and rich sensory motor tracts for movement? Do you have a constitution that was made to confront, to hunt, to withstand physical acts? Does your body's mind image action? If yes to these, you are a MESOMORPH.

Were you born with long bones, long fingers, a small head? Are you a sensor, an alert attender, with a rich sensory network of nerves, continually accumulating data? Are you a plotter, a planner, a trapper, who senses and penetrates situations? If so, you are an ECTOMORPH.

Were you born a pear-shaped person who makes use of what is? A powerhouse of determination? Are you big gutted; do you enjoy bringing people together? Are you slow moving, short legged, and enduring? You are an ENDOMORPH.

Embodied myths are ways of being alive

Your embodied shape determines your form of aliveness.

Ectomorphs live from the surface of the skin's receptor nerves and from an enlarged network of central nervous tissue – the web of eyes, ears, tongue, nose, joints, and organs. Sensory stimuli form a pointillistic painting, an image of self and of the world. An ectomorph tries to maintain sensory contact without being overwhelmed by the outside world. He seeks to deepen embodiment, attached yet separate. The ectomorph is the lonesome cowboy, the misunderstood recluse, the image maker.

Mesomorphs generates excitement through physical action – doing, performing, self-testing. They take their power from their muscles and midbrain. They experience their aliveness by being physically active. The endomorph lives by his or her appetite, for sensuousness and for keeping company. The endo has a big soma, appetite seeking contact.

Your myth and the pattern of society

These patterns of embodiment are our inner life story, the story of our bodied self. But these patterns may conflict with the patterns of a society that demands that we be what society needs. In our society, for example, you are taught to be independent, rational, logical, self-controlled. Power is to be found not in nature, but in objective – and objectifying – fact-finding. But the function of fact-finding distances you from the emotional matrix that you live in. It distances you from your own subjective truth, which is nonrational as well as rational.

Everyone's endomorphic myth

From out of the great somatic collective, from the genetic code, comes the story of our basic identity, our predisposition to respond to the world in a particular way. The somatic unconscious, the realm of the unknown body, the generative abundance, is endomorphic. From this layer of our body come the myths of creation, the earth as Great Mother, even the theory of evolution, our coming from the ocean.

Before the emergence of very powerful, mesomorphic hunters, we lived surrounded by an abundance of nature. We engaged in food gathering. There was no separateness between ourselves and our environment.

One somatic image that reflects that life is the Venus of Olendorf: big hips, big breasts – the symbols of the fertility and the abundance of existence. This image is part of our structure, part of our somatic unconsciousness. It is the endomorph in all of us. It appears in our dreams, visions, and loving relationships.

All of us grew in our mother's belly – the Garden of Eden, a part of everybody's earliest experience. The endomorphic myth is founded in our earliest body experience.

The mesomorphic myths

That first myth is followed by the active self-determining myths of the mesomorphic phase. The mesomorphic age is filled with the stories of hunters and warriors.

The urges of life

There are other myths and somatic images that express the urges of life. We take our roles from those myths and images. Myths about being Dionysian. About the loyalty of Parsifal. Myths about controlling nature, being influenced by our own nature. There are myths about transforming nature – the stories of alchemy, or the stories of romanticism. These are myths of awakening, creation, self-formation. They speak of the body's ability to imitate roles, to make them part of oneself. We find in myths characters that resonate within themselves, and we use myths to create order out of our own experience.

The mythic age today

In human history, we have lived through the endomorphic mythological age. We have passed through a mesomorphic inheritance as well, forging change. Now we have begun to explore the ectomorphic, the role of the individual. These ectomorphs are information gatherers, researchers, sensory farmers, digital visual actors, who live in images and a disembodied reality. We aspire to images of what should be. We are like Giacometti sculptures, bodies without an inside, dimensionless silhouettes.

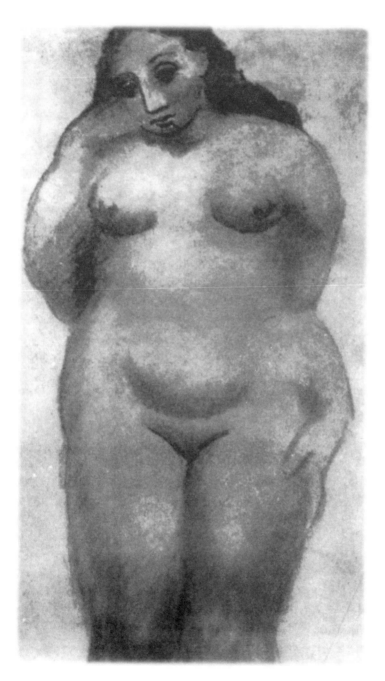

PABLO PICASSO, "NUDE WOMAN STANDING," 1906

GEORGES BRAQUE, "LARGE NUDE," 1908

PART TWO

Entering the Formative Life

Sing in me, Muse, and through me tell the story
of that man skilled in all ways of contending.

– HOMER, *Odyssey*
translation by Robert Fitzgerald

CHAPTER 3

The Wasteland

OUR GOAL as individual bodied beings is to manifest the somatic process as a mythic experience. When we lose our somatic reality, we inhabit a Wasteland: the myth of the abandoned body. To be filled again is the Grail.

STANLEY KELEMAN

There's been such a rapid transformation in our social and economic life contacts – it changes so fast now – that nothing is stabilized, and you have to do it yourself. You have to fight through this uninterpreted field to discover your own mythic interpretation. That is a challenge. It's a hard one, but it can be done. If you realize that in your life work you might be in an archetypal role of some kind, and play it that way, it's a much more informing view of ourselves. Without it, we're in a wasteland.

Joseph Campbell

Abandonment

At one time I almost abandoned myself, the vital and emotional street person, the immigrants' son, to become an overrational and objectifying. As I engaged in the pursuit of mental excitement, I did not know that I was stunting myself. When I found my way back to my somatic inheritance, I began to live from my body's aliveness, to form a life from what I had been given. Being embodied, I learned that I could make a personal life from the nonpersonal somatic process. I learned that the Wasteland had to do with abandoning, or being cut off from, the bodied life.

We have abandoned the body for rationality and language, symbols and signs. The brain has organized a reality of image and thought, venerating the invisible life of consciousness. We exist in a Wasteland where images feed off the soma's vitality, where thought is in love with its own reflection. We are wandering in the desert, thirsting and parched because the deep waters of the soma are no longer available to us. We live in the Wasteland, where our bodies exist for the sole purpose of the mind.

Objectifying the body

If we see our body as a thing, if we see it only as an objective biological process, we fail to understand our inward form of being embodied. We turn our somatic interior into an outside; we objectify ourselves. As bodied beings, we subjectively know the divine, the eternal protoplasmic organizing process. To be present in our life bodily is to be of the animate earth. To live as an image is to be in a Wasteland.

The body has become a victim of its own imaging process gone haywire. The body has a wonderful facility for organizing complex images and concepts, arranging them to give a personal order. We use the brain to make an object of our own body. This imaging process was meant originally to organize experience. Now it has taken the place of bodily experience. Using our imaging process in that way, we have destroyed the basis of our tissue consciousness.

Mythology talks about organizing experience: about our origins as a living process, about how to preserve the experience of our ancestors. It makes stories about our place in the world and our place in a local time continuum. But at a certain point, the ability to form images, and then symbols, begins to take us over. The symbol's meaning becomes a substitute for the experience itself.

The human body is an archetype

Our basic animating pattern is an archetype. The human body, an ancient body pattern, is always present. The pattern is not only the upright human form; it is also the basic excitatory pattern we experience as the urge to replicate, to be close, to herd, to nurse, to care for others. Through this pattern we empathize with all living creatures; we feel an identity with them. In the foreground of our life, we know the body as personal form; we live it as family myth. "Be like your uncle, the priest, the philosopher." Or as society's myth. "Be civil, be rational." We are both ancient and modern.

The idealized image

When we idealize image instead of bodily experience, we find ourselves living in the image. Now most of society is organized in ways that set it apart from its own nature. Nature itself has become an image, an idea, a symbol, a picture in the brain – and so has the body. We live in the image of the body, not in the body.

Direct and indirect experience

We live in two realms: the realm of direct experience and the realm of representative images. Being able to live in both realms and being able to conduct a dialogue between them is the very nature of somatic existence. There is no duality then – only a recognition of two different realms. What has happened is that we have mistaken one realm for the other; and in so doing, we have lost touch with the body. The image – not the body – has become our direct experience.

Freud and nature

It is not commonly realized that Freud put nature inside the person. This made for a gigantic change in the field of perception, but it went unnoticed for fifty years. Until Freud, nature was outside. You walked in the woods, and you saw nature, and you had a relationship with the natural world. After Freud, all of a sudden talk was no longer about a relationship with nature, but about nature in the form of the unconscious, in the form of the libido inside you. Today nature is no longer "out there"; it is in you. With that shift in our experience of nature, we begin to experience the body as the brain's images. These images replace the somatic experience. Where once we understood image through experience, now we understand the experience only by what its symbols mean.

The need for images

As you move away from the vitality of experience, you need the images intensified to a high degree in order to evoke an adrenalized response – to make you feel alive, to make you feel your roles. Because you don't see those roles played out in the natural world anymore. Why are the images in our head so precious to us? Originally, they expressed a way of knowing what was going on inside us, of relating to our inner experience. The images in our brain served as an inner connection. Now this function of the brain has been idolized to such a degree that we have lost sight of its source.

Images and distancing

Today we regard the images that come from the brain as if they were creation itself. We regard images as if they were reality. We create an image and then say we are the image. The image the body makes, then, is who we are. We are in love with the images in our body's mind; we do not know the body itself directly.

As we live the excitement of our brain's images, the body distances itself from its own emotional and somatic experience. Since we do not experience the natural body, we become addicted to images to stimulate us, to make us feel alive. We have blurred the distinction between mental experience and organic experience. This difference makes of our world a Wasteland.

Experience and the body

Experience is part of the body's self-organizing process, a pattern of response by which the body knows what is, and what is on the way to becoming. In that sense, the flux of experience as emotions, movements, sensations, creates an anatomic image in the brain of what is going on, or what has already happened. The body's responses make an anatomic image, and then an auditory or visual image; they go together. When they are split off from each other, we live in images without a body. Or we live as a body without images of itself.

The basic experience of the body is its pulses, which organize multiple realities in layers of expanding and gathering; of fullness and emptiness. This process generates two times: the time of the event and the time of the response, of encoding the event. The duration of the event and its organizational imprint, which is the present and past, take place in the same person. We maintain in our tissue the actual event, and an organization of an image of the event. Out of one event we have organized the experiential and the symbolic.

Maturity from the Wasteland

Our body generates separate aspects of an experience, with different time frames. But in our secular culture, we dismiss the soma's subjective sense of time. We identify it as the shadowy dream time. We try to give it a reality by assigning a social meaning to its images. When we do this, we are trying to objectify a process, rather than live from it. When we begin to be intimate with the pulse and quality of somatic experience, we begin to appreciate this experience as myth, outside of objective time; as myth that forms internal knowing. As we learn to live again from our organic responses, the soma grows itself, deepens its feelings and images. In this way we grow a maturity out of the Wasteland.

CHAPTER 4

Body as Image, Experience, and Somatic Imagination

WHAT I HAVE come to recognize is that the body grows its vision of the future. The kid tells you what kind of man he wants to be when he grows up. "I want to be a fireman." But the fact of the matter is that we grow to be what our body wants us to be. The somatic image is directly related to the biological process.

I am speaking only of those images which come from the body's own process, not those imposed by society. Desire can be an image in your brain or an image in action. If desire is not bodied, there is no expression and response. The soma's desire organizes an image of action.

STANLEY KELEMAN

∽

Campbell: I have a recollection in my own history that is a rather important one. In my last years at college, my real interests were playing in a jazz band and track athletics. Music and athletics were what I was really dealing with. Then I became fascinated by the Arthurian romances and their relation to the mythological material I had been interested in as a kid. I knew if I were going to follow that through and really get the juice of it, these other activities would drop off. They dropped off like part of an eggshell. Then I went to Europe as a scholar, studying at the university, getting clues as to how to study this material that I was excited about. I wasn't doing it for anybody else.

In Paris, I was sitting in the garden of Cluny. I had spent a year on the philological material of old French grammar related to medieval Latin. It suddenly came over me: I don't give a damn about the laws for the etymology of words as they move from Latin into old French and Provencal. The thing that is really gripping me in this material is the mythological material. With that decision, I dropped the Ph.D., dropped the whole thing. It never touched me. It was a life decision, but it was a life decision made in a choice of images. Are these images of this way of scholarship amounting to experience for me, or is it simply something that I am putting on to get a reward of a Ph.D. degree? Or am I going to follow my star?

Keleman: But the somatic organizations of the musician, the runner, are still with you, present in your image as a person. They still play a part in forming your decisions.

Campbell: Those were things I was living.

Keleman: You never gave them up. It is so obvious and evident that you are still the runner in the way you move, even to this day. I can talk about it in terms of your memory. I can talk about it as somatic organization to excel, the hardening of the body to win. That is all present in the image Joe Campbell shows the world. The specific activity has been given up, but that emotional-somatic form is present in you. It is present in the shape of your body, in how you move, in how you transfer that experience from one area of interest to another. How would you get rid of your body image of the runner?

Those images of the doctoral student, on the other hand, were not fully somatized for you. You began by exploring somebody else's image about how to study. But when you were excited, you reoriented yourself toward a different goal. You mobilized an image called scholar. You began to mobilize it when you had an emotional mental image: "Hey, wait a minute. This is how I will use myself. I am going to embody that vision." The impulse formed Joseph Campbell, the scholar who ran into the forest of mythology to search for the Grail, to listen to the music of the ancient adventure.

From our experience comes an inner somatic image. This image may conflict with the life-structuring somatic images that society imposes. In your case, those images did not stimulate innate experience. When society imposes an image that is not related to our body's visceral depth, it is not embodied deeply. Society's images are meant to use our body's vitality; if we are cut off from our own emotions, the external images do not live in us. They are disembodied.

∽

Two images

A physician friend of mine told me about an experience he had while he was in the hospital being treated for cardiac arrhythmia. A device that was attached to a TV camera took pictures of his heart. In a moment of shock, he realized that what he was looking at was his heart. He was amazed to see his heart fibrillating while he felt the irregular beat in his chest. There were two images: the visual cardiac image in front of his nose and the pattern of beats in his chest that did not feel right.

I remarked to my friend that the pain he had felt when he entered the hospital was on his face, and the way he clutched his chest was an image that alerted the doctor to be concerned and to act. My friend agreed. His inner organ had begun to act unpredictably; the heartbeat did not match the neural image in his brain. Nor did the sensations in his chest match the sensation pattern that he had established as his norm.

In this story we have image as a visual pattern, an organ pattern, an emotional pattern, and a means of communication. We have a somatic image generated from internal pain that acts as an emotional image for ourselves and for others. One image is in our brain. The other is in the body as a whole, in the tissues of the organs of communication.

The beat of the heart is a continuous pulse, an animate, motile, anatomic image. The image the heart makes in its beating is recognized by the tissue around it. The body around the heart responds to the heartbeat pattern just as other people respond when image becomes an emotional expression. Somatic image is a process organized by the organism as a way to communicate with itself.

Inherited image

Our somatic process organizes its own inherited images. It organizes the image of the human body – two-armed, two-legged, two-eyed, standing erect. It organizes different body images: the youth, the adult, the aging adult. All of these shapes communicate to others. The somatic process also organizes shapes that give personal expression to our body. We have the inherited nakedness that announces our gender – the image of our maleness or femaleness – for all to see. We have personal contractions and postures that hide, out of shame or fear, our basic body image. Fear, lust, joy, pride, sympathy – all are part of the soma's images, as is internal pain or the expression of expectation, and our internal personal shape as poet, singer, lover. Image is a living structure.

Inherited plan and shape

Every living organism has an inherited plan for its growth, replication, differentiation, and shape. This plan, or code pattern, and the body shapes that accompany it, are organic images; images of past events that are still present and images for the future that are not yet bodied. Embryological growth, with its dramatic shapes, which appear quickly and change just as quickly into other shapes – from blastula, to embryo, to fetus, to infant – manifests that inherited plan. The organic images that organize, assemble, and maintain our shape are what I call somatic images.

Volitional gestures: the willful smile

The organism's ability to preserve its responses and make them part of our ongoing process is partly volitional. This ability of the body's brain to influence its own body image gives us a personal bodied self. To show the image of tenderness – the smile – is nonvolitional; to be able to repeat it is volitional. To repeat the gesture of tenderness is to enhance the body's relationships and its growth.

The somatic process is a reservoir of inherited shapes, of body and behavioral images from the past. We, as present living beings, are connected to the parade of ancestral shapes. We inherit our ancestors and live them in the present. Living is the process of realizing and growing our inherited and personal image.

The study of humans is the study of the process of embodiment. From the body's process we discover our inward cosmos – the feelings, images, and sounds that organize our personal behavior.

The stability of shape and pattern

An image, for me, is the same as a pattern. It is a cellular organization, a complex, specific somatic shape. Our body shape is an image of our animal and personal body. Shape, as image, has duration and is relatively stable. It is bodily organization in slow motion. Conversely, a pattern of movement is also a shape. How a cell or an animal moves, then, is a pattern that forms an image that we recognize. Our senses recognize these moving shapes in space. The body also recognizes its own inner organ motility, its moving images of itself. These inner and outer motile organizations are, for me, somatic images and are the basis of our self-identity.

Natural and imitable shapes

There are also somatic-emotional images – the scowling face, the clenched fist, the depressive shrinking. We react to these emotional images in others as others react to them in us. We respond with our own somatic emotional image – we scowl, we smile ingratiatingly, or whatever. Finally, there are somatic images that arise from our inherited genetic pattern – the meso, endo, or ecto body shapes. Some somatic images arise naturally. But others are formed through imitation. It is not easy to make body patterns from our internal feelings, to give those feelings an external expression. These are formative acts. That is why we admire and imitate artists, actors, athletes.

Our modern myth is about the decoding of creation, the understanding of the genetic code. Our creation myth is also the myth of our biological evolution. For me, there is another aspect to the creation and evolution myth – that is, the coming into existence of the body's subjectivity. Myth seems to speak to internal somatic states. For me, myth is about the birth and evolution of the body's inner subjective experience.

Embryogenesis is cosmogenesis; the birth of the body is the birth of the inner emotional cosmos. And the experience of this is still ongoing, is present now. From the moment of our conception, the organizing of our past somatic images is available to us as a guide for being in the world in the present.

The parent of somatic images is the body's process of to make form and expression. And this process extends back through the layers of our evolutionary history. The series of bodies we have organized and lived in our personal embodiment – the infant, the adolescent, the adult – is the long body. The long body is also the genetic shapes we have inherited from our ancestors' body forms, be it ecto, meso, endo. We have the caveman in us as well as the modern man.

The long body

The long body is the chain of bodies we are part of. The human is an amalgamation of the parade of somatic images. The different bodies of our history – personal and impersonal – are in our dreams. Myth presents us also with the body images of various ages and eons. The complex of somatic images gives our present somatic image an organization and a dimension, a structure that has duration.

The long body is the parade of the bodies that we have had from the onset of human conception. These bodies exist now not as memory, but as structure. They are still there, functioning. It is one body laid next to another body, so to speak. Mostly we are in touch with the surface body, because perception is mostly a surface phenomenon. That doesn't mean that the other bodies aren't there.

We are more than a biochemical process, and certainly not a machine. Or a chemical arrangement, a physiological arrangement that just accidentally developed a functional form. The soma is an ecological system, like the earth. One layer of life, old but very much part of the present; environments in a configuration. When you say "my body," you are talking about a collage of environments, an organized somatic world, that all says "me."

In FINNEGAN'S WAKE there is a beautiful thing about the long body. Joyce has the image of the Liffey as the heroine of the book. This river rises in the mountains south of Dublin as a dancing, twinkling little girl, streams coming together in a joyous way. Then she flows westward a little way and then northward through the suburban areas – a rather lovely part of the areas around Dublin – as a young woman, and then as the matron, the mother, the image of the household. Then she turns eastward and flows out through Dublin as a rather dirty city stream, gathering all the filth of the city and carrying it out to sea.

Once out to sea, she joins her father Ocean again, and the sun lifts the vapor, forming clouds in her blue womb heaven, and then the clouds come over the Whitlow hills and release the water, and you have them fall to the earth and start again. Those are all the stages of a woman's life, but they are all there simultaneously. Even though you happen to be in the Whitlow hills, and then you go to Dublin, and then you go out into the country, you see different stages of that life, as though that's the way it were now. But it is all there together; all stages exist simultaneously.

We are a process of somatic images – some of our external body, some inside the body, the continuity of the images. Even in your childhood, your old age is there waiting for you.

Joseph Campbell

Behavior is part of a library

Behavior is a complex of somatic images. We are a library of moving images. These images are part of the somatic psyche. As adults, there are times when we are primitive man; other times when we are a rational parent who is in control. Sometimes there are expressions that have no frame of reference.

To work with the body as a process is to see that the soma's expressions have a structure, and that this structure is a complex of images. These innate or learned emotional and social images are a behavior and a way to communicate one's intentions to oneself and others. By engaging these patterns of expression, we begin to organize other body images, as the stabilized rigid structure becomes more motile.

World view and your somatic-emotional structure

When a person tells a dream that has personal meaning for him, or relates a myth that he associates with his dilemma, I notice the pattern of gesturing or the somatic posture he is using. These expressions are part of how one expresses complicated emotions. I identify these emotional images and try to determine whether they are innate or learned.

Say that I notice a stiff upper body and neck. This stiffness seems to come from an attitude of reserve or fear. I wonder: Is this reserve an image learned at home to show deference? Or is it the withholding that signals fear of coming close or being overwhelmed by one's excitement? One is an innate fear image, the other is a learned social posture and image. Both images signal to the person who has organized them that he is in this state of reserve or fear. Both images also tell others of his state. The somatic-emotional image is meant to establish a relationship with self or others.

When I suggest that the person exaggerate this stiffness, that he do it more intensely, the emotional image becomes more vivid. This exaggeration can then be diminished, shifting the image to a less intense organization. Fear becomes caution; reserve becomes shyness. As we do this back and forth, images become more motile. This method, which I speak about in a later chapter, helps the soma to differentiate its library of possible innate and learned emotional images. The practice makes it evident that our body process is an image maker.

If you work somatically with a person's emotional images, tensing, you shift the way that person recognizes himself. As a result, he may feel disoriented or anxious. He loses his sense of his body. If another somatic-emotional image is not embodied and made stable, the sense of personal continuity is disrupted. We tend to want to maintain our present somatic image, because we dread the unsureness that comes before the stabilizing of a new one.

Our somatic structure determines how we perceive the world. It determines that we be in the world in our particular way. When you work with people somatically, they retell their experiences in a completely different way than they did before. Their experiences of how they are (for example, with their spouse) alter dramatically. People's structures change, depending on whether they are lying down or standing.

I have never known a client to perceive a dream the same way lying down and sitting up. You ask a client to tell you his dream in one somatic stance. Then after you work bodily, you ask him to tell you the dream again. The person, after changing his somatic stance, has a whole new set of associations from which he is deriving meaning. All of a sudden he is a participant in the dream. You can actually watch him shift between these two modes as he changes somatic stance.

On the basis of this, I would say that a person's world view depends on how he is somatically-emotionally structured. So if you inhibit yourself from responding to emotional, bodily information, you get one kind of world view. If you let yourself respond, you get another kind, because you have altered your experience of self in the world.

CHAPTER 5

The Siren's Call: The Authentic and the Inauthentic Life

SOCIETY TODAY believes that you can be all you want to be. The mind's image dominates. You find the role to play and change and diminish your own somatic image; you turn it into something "better." But my point is to experience your somatic image, to know it as something you've organized from inside.

STANLEY KELEMAN

Keleman: Images that are grounded in the soma are authentic. When we live concepts and images that are not grounded in our body, we do not believe in who we are. When the body loses contact with its own interior somatic image, we are alienated from the sacred. The hero of Woody Allen's film, *Zelig,* is an unformed adult who takes his identity from famous people. He has no sense of himself; he borrows other people's identity. He thinks he can be anybody. Actually, he is without body.

Campbell: These two terms: image and experience. Out of an experience, one may create an image that becomes a governor for action, that moves into action. In a traditional society, the images to which you are to respond are given you. And they may not constitute operative images. The image is just there, and you're really not experiencing it. I had a term for an operative mythological image – that it is an energy-evoking and directing sign. If it doesn't hit the energy centers, you've got nothing happening.

Not only is image generated from inside, but images are found outside. One of the intentions of a mythological system is to present evocative images, images that touch and resonate in very deep centers of our impulse system, and then move us from those very deep centers into action.

A traditional society supplies all the images that you are supposed to respond to. The mythology might be regarded as a net or web of models. But in our world, the thing is broken wide open. A lot of exotic images come in. This whole matter of the discovered image to which the individual resonates seems to me to be a very important feature in education, the pedagogical image. That is, the teacher, the coach, or whoever it is who is in a position of teaching, becomes himself or herself a model for the student. And when you don't have mature humans teaching, you don't have very effective imitative or growth-stimulating models. That is just the beginning.

The image that is provided asks for a life-generating response on the part of the person viewing it. Ideally, an image is presented that evokes energies from various intended centers of the psyche. Let's say it serves as a kind of magnet to draw certain systems of energy, and so to provide a life-building, suggestive structure, so that you build your life toward this. Today, what they provide is not the sort of thing that is provided by a fine teacher or a noble person. A youngster at school just sees the body of some great athlete and says, "Gee, I want to have a body like that."

In the traditional society, all sorts of models are provided. In our society we have to do it for ourselves.

Keleman: What makes us believe we know how to somatize an image from inside, how to embody it? My assumption is that most of us are operating by imitating external images. We have lost contact with our own interior somatic image, and with the process of organizing an image into an act.

Let us say that a myth suggests ways to act in a specific situation. The mythological world expresses the struggle of the primary subcortical reflex trying to maintain the inner environment and find a way to maintain its body metabolism and shape in the face of unusual encounters. In this struggle, the subcortical brain depends upon its cortical brain to define and refine immediate reflex responses. This inner dialogue between an inherited routine organization and its cortical brain organizes a contemporary behavior.

In contemporary society, information and facts and brain images of how to be are taken as real, and myth and somatic response are treated as make-believe. If you ask how a person should be, you get a scientific study on how one should eat. Or you get a statistical survey of what sexual activity should be, rather than insights into the deep subcortical processes that prime the somatic, erotic imagination. In the formative concept, the subcortical brain and the cortical centers co-operate to organize body behavior. In contemporary society, information and the senses of sight and sound impose images that suppress or dominate the subcortical self. And so we modern people are banished from Eden to live only in the cortical images of the brain. The constitutional images and vitality of the subcortex are subdued.

In the old cultures, we deeply believed in myths and visions, in telling stories about how to experience, how to use our bodies. The society used song, dance, and religious rituals to support these mythic images of the body, and the experiences it wished people to have.

The human brain and the viscera have the ability to generate image. The brain learns to use this image to influence its behavior. The heartbeat, the continuing peristalsis of the intestine, the pulse, and muscle tonus produce sensations that the brain organizes into a neural image, and then a pictorial image.

Our body makes an image of itself in its brain. This is called body image or somatic image. How our body's emotional expression appears to others is also a somatic image. Mythology hands down images, such as the scholar, the priest, the servant. When we live by these disembodied images or somatic poses – roles that are not grounded in our body's emotions – they lack the emotional power to sustain us. These images are inauthentic because they are poorly bodied.

Our body has an innate ability to influence itself from its emotional experience. In every civilization, there have been rituals and images that enable us to do this. We use those images as models. The inner-outer dialogue generated by these models helps us to form a personal subjectivity: a set of perceptions and a collection of muscle movements that we can volitionally link to behavior.

All of us engage in this process every day of our lives, whether we know it or not. Most of us don't know how we try to manipulate ourselves into being liked, into being more womanly, being more manly. We try to live an image, which we believe ourselves to be. Most of us think that we are manipulating our minds. But in fact, one part of the body is manipulating another part.

C.G. Jung saw myth as part of the biological matrix. I define myth as originating from our tissue's cells, a nonlinear image that is governed by the body's metabolism. There is a pulse that initiates natural rhythms and tides of light, such as you see in dreams – a world where people have different shapes and time is kaleidoscopic and collapsible. And it is from this basic cellular process that our internal images come to the fore as somatic patterns: the warrior or the wise man; the Great Mother or the Amazon.

These somatic shapes are embedded in the genetic structure. Plato called them archetypes. The Greeks anthropomorphized these great forces in human form, their pantheon of gods and goddesses. They gave that force a god's name. So that you could say, "That man has in him the sea god, the upwelling of tides and hormones, and excitatory storms." Or, "That man is angry and volatile and unpredictable, like Zeus." These body behavior patterns were seen in nature, and human nature was seen as bodying nature.

> *Campbell:* Myth and the body. Myth and nature. Our mind makes myth not from its own rational programs, but in response to suggestions from the body as to what is needed.
>
> This image, pedagogical force of image, where does the image come from? Who provides it? Who responds to it? Why is it that a whole galaxy of images can be presented, but only one work?

What is that? Another image will be grabbing someone sitting right beside you. These recognitions of your own response system are so important.

Keleman: The life of the body is the source of our myths. Oswald Spengler, in *The Decline of the West,* talks about the ages of a culture – spring, summer, autumn, winter – and its life forms. This holds true for the life of the organism, as biological and social self, and for our personal life cycle. This is the stuff of myth, the somatic story. Myth has to do with the movement of our universal and personal body.

Biology is a mythology, and when one wades through all the anatomic and physiologic information, one is reading science's myths of what it means to be human. And what it means, it seems, is that the body is a machine, an overrational, objectifying Frankenstein, that can be programmed to be civil or murderous.

Society today believes that you can be all you want to be. The mind's image dominates. You find the role to play and change and diminish your own somatic image; you turn it into something "better." But my point is to experience your somatic image, to know it as something you've organized from inside. You become intimate with its structure and you know how the somatic process maintains us in a continuity throughout our life. That is the first step.

In society today we are practicing bodying somebody's manu-factured image about how humans should be. We should be powerful, sexy. I should look and act like this type of man, this type of woman. So we start to practice bodying that external image; we deny our own somatic imagination. What image am I practicing to be? What image have I practiced to be? And, of course, what image is trying to take form from my own body?

Campbell: We can call an image a primary mask or an anti-thetical mask. The primary mask would be the system of images that the society puts on you, to which you are supposed to respond. For instance, the kind of boy you are supposed to be, and then finding out the kind of little boy you are. There is a difference there between the given image of the society and the potential image that is coming up inside. Sometimes you have to go way back to find what the real images were in the operating and shaping of your life. They were not those given by society.

Some of the images that the society gives you as models may take; you may actually operate in that way. Others will not, in which case you fake it. Then your life becomes, in a sense, an inauthentic life, or a cultural life. This is one of the themes of the Grail legend, what is called the Wasteland theme. Wolfram von Eschenbach does it most wonderfully. His point is that in the twelfth and early thirteenth centuries, people for the most part were living inauthentic lives. They were professing beliefs they didn't have, they were marrying people they had never seen before, and professing and trying to experience love. People who hadn't really the qualifications for the job that they were holding. Representatives of the spiritual life in the church were not really people of spiritual format of any kind. The whole thing was a fake. The discontinuity between nature and the image of society was so radical that the thing was in dissolution, and within two hundred years it had broken up.

How can one bring this Wasteland back to life again? By being someone with what the Middle Ages called a gentle or noble heart, a person of deep and rich sensibilities to live authentically. Not obeying, but living out of the spontaneity of compassion, and honesty. This would restore the world, it would be fruitful. This is to eat from the Tree of Life again.

These are two images that in a way, I think, establish what we're dealing with here. The mask you put over yourself, the moral notions of how you think you should be. Or your pride in how you should be. And then you find that within yourself a snotty little boy or nasty little girl was living, and would be snotty or nasty if you let it come through. It wouldn't be something experienced only as negative.

You can put on a social image or mask, and live in reaction to that all the time, judging yourself on the basis of the primary mask system. That is absolutely all that you are allowed in the traditionally functioning social order. But in our world, it is open. You are capable of bringing out the authenticity of your own potential.

Which image is the actual operative one? The one that has been given you and which you haven't really matched to your own experience system? Or the one that really has grown on your experience and has given you an image to move toward, like a pedagogical image?

A lot of people who teach are utterly bored with it, but they do it because it is going to give them a position in this club, the academic club. The teaching is dry, and they are dry, and they are bored. I know tons of them; you probably do, too. These are people who did something that they did not directly experience at all. They experienced it as their duty, to be done in a dry way. It is put upon them. Your own experience in literature, in life – have you let a life build out of that? Bumping against the difficulties that come from not doing the things that you are supposed to do?

What if we choose not to do the things we are supposed to do? The principal gain is a sense of an authentic act – and an authentic life. It may be a short one, but it is an authentic one, and that's a lot better than those short lives full of boredom. The principal loss is security. Another is respect from the community. But you gain the respect of another community, the one that is worth having the respect of. You will perhaps lose a lovely, orderly life with things coming in at traditional times and at traditional places. You will cut off part of you.

It was Abraham Maslow who found a list of gains that the general, dime-a-dozen type live for. They are survival, security, prestige, social relations, ego development. When I read that, I thought, "The person who really sees through the image, sees something to live for, will sacrifice every one of those five without a thought." This is in a sense the words of Jesus: "He who loses his life will find it; he who finds his life will lose it." That is what he's talking about. Give up the life that is put on you. Follow your own thing. Then you are in that wonderful image of the place with the dark forest, in a place that you have chosen where there is no way or path. When you're on the path of someone else, you've lost your life.

Keleman: The body is the source of its own images. It fabricates them, like a clothes manufacturer. And they're in your head and in the muscular patterns. "I'm going to be successful." It's one thing to think that thought and then to copy someone. "I see that he's a student; I'm going to be a student." I borrow that image from the outside. But in order to actually do something – read, write – I have to sit down to pick up the book, and pick up the pencil. I have to use myself. And now *I've* generated that image. I have a direct experiential representation in my brain and body to refer to for shorthand.

Campbell: When does myth become effective as the body, and when does it not? When does the earth become an operating image, the structures of a life process? That is really what we're talking about here. I think your word is a rather good one. The happening, or an experience, the myth, can just be a happening, something that is presented to you, and it is not yours. But what myth are you living? What are the images of your structuring process?

When does the psyche take the role in and turn it into a life-structuring form, out of which one then acts almost with spontaneity? It becomes part of one's spontaneity, transforming the Wasteland. What have been your spontaneities in the past, that stay with you all the way through? They are a part of that continually growing organic structure. It's a great idea. It's something to take it, then put it together with what we think of as our experience, and then reorganize our relationship to it.

ALBERTO GIACOMETTI, "MAN CROSSING THE STREET"
41

PABLO PICASSO, "LE MENEUR DE CHEVAL," 1905
© 1999 Estate of Pablo Picasso / Artists Rights Society (ARS), New York

PART THREE

The Hero's Journey:
The Somatic Unconscious

The hero's myth is about the growth
and the subjectivity of an adult.

PABLO PICASSO, "BOY LEADING A HORSE," 1906
© 1999 Estate of Pablo Picasso / Artists Rights Society (ARS), New York

CHAPTER 6

Parsifal:
A Formative Myth of the West

❧

The changing body of the hero

The hero's journey begins with conception. The hero becomes an adult who forms many shapes. This quest is formative throughout life. How the hero used himself in situations that were challenging becomes the theme of myths. The tales are about how it's possible to use oneself physically, emotionally, and imaginatively to organize the three layers we inherit – ecto, meso, endo. And then to share our experiences with others.

The modern hero

The hero's myth is about embodiment. It shows us how to learn the lessons of our embodiment as we overcome obstacles, challenges, and changes. The tradition started at the dawn of Western civilization with the Sumerian myth of the mesomorphic hero Gilgamesh, as it began to replace the endomorphic myth of the Great Mother. The mesomophic hero continues his appearance in Homer's *Odyssey*. Then, in the Bible, the ectomorphic heroes Moses and Jesus, who also believed in a disembodied God, deny biological inheritance.

Parsifal, a story from the Middle Ages, is about the emergence and growth of individuality and romantic love. Parsifal represents a trinity – the reappearance of the endomorph hero integrated with the ectomorph and mesomorph.

The hero becomes an embodied individual

Parsifal's tale is an adventure story about becoming a complex individual. Like Parsifal, we struggle to live with oppositions and contradictions in order to organize compassion, action, and knowledge. We begin to form a deeper somatic reality, which includes unity and love. The legend of Parsifal is also about somatic individuality – the organizing of the ectomorphic, mesomorphic, and endomorphic layers into a new individual.

The developmental body

One can follow the story of Parisfal's change in body growth. In the early part of his life, he is attracted by the image and social code of knighthood. This image inspires him and provides his call to adventure. The image of knighthood influence his body from the outside to do what he thinks he should do. Living by an image is an ectomorphic function.

Parsifal then begins to dramatize his way of being in the world. This is the mesomorphic function. He follows the code of knighthood and lives out the warrior drama.

A significant event in his story is the refusal of Parsifal's brother to kill Parsifal. Parsifal is shown compassion – and this is the initiation of the endomorphic function. The final shape Parsifal incorporates is that of the endomorph.

The formative storyline

These three bodies of the hero did not become integrated of their own accord. It required volitional effort. This effort can be looked at as a series of steps:

STEP ONE.

The hero is aroused by an event or an image. For Parsifal, it is the image of knighthood.

STEP TWO.

Parsifal begins to use his body as a knight, as he imagines what a knight is. He tries on the shape of the knight and warrior. All the trials, all the wars, all the journeys serve but one purpose: to establish and live out the body of the warrior, the gentleman warrior, the social warrior.

STEP THREE.

The shape of the warrior begins to be inappropriate. Events tell that Parsifal he must change. This stage of the story includes being asked to leave the Grail Castle. He is still bound by the codes of others. He does not know how to receive, be compassionate, be his own individual, his own shape, his own person. As this code becomes less useful, Parsifal begins to disorganize his attitude. As Parsifal disorganizes the warrior stance, he is able to receive kindness and share it.

STEP FOUR.

Parsifal's willingness to suppport compassion changes his shape. As his shape changes, new qualities emerge. In this story what emerges is compassion and empathy.

To receive somebody, you have to allow them a place in you and respond to it. It requires a pliability and tenderness rather than hardness. To contain another's situation as well as your own is to be another kind of hero. The knights called it amour. We call it empathy.

STEP FIVE.

This new body shape – a shape that is now compassion – is a man who understands, empathizes and embraces. It is tough as well as protective. Parsifal returns to the Grail Castle and brings about a reconciliation between himself and the ailing king.

The Grail represents a high
symbol of spiritual fulfillment.
Joseph Campbell

To use yourself differently
is the key to your salvation.
Never mind changing the old man,
the Grail King, who lacks the fulfillment
necessary for his position.
No, the answer remains with Parsifal.
The old man is affected by how Parsifal uses himself.

STANLEY KELEMAN

The Legend of Parsifal

RETOLD BY JOSEPH CAMPBELL

The Grail King has been wounded. As a result of this wound, a curse lies over the whole land. The main theme of the Grail romance is the existence of a land laid waste, which must be brought to life again.

The wounded inauthentic life

The King Anfortas (that is, in French, "the infirm one") is a beautiful young man, and he did not earn the role of Lord of the Grail and the Grail Castle. He inherited it. He has not, in his own life, experienced the fulfillment of his position. As he is riding forward, there comes out of the forest before him a pagan knight. This knight is from Islam, from the Holy Land, and represents nature. These two ride at each other and the

pagan knight is killed. Nature man is killed by the Christian lance. But the lance of the pagan knight castrates the king. This idea of the supernatural against natural grace has castrated nature. Contemporary Europe's nature is of the Wasteland. Its nature does not come from the body, from the heart, but from some ideal laid upon you.

The king goes back to the castle with the head of the lance still in the wound. When the head is removed, on it is written the word "Grail." The sense of that is that the highest spiritual aim is implicit in the dynamism of nature. The Grail Knight is going to have to be one who acts according to his nature, to the nature of a noble heart. The knight who is the candidate doesn't know it. It is Parsifal.

The inherited body

Parsifal's father is a knight errant. His name is Gahmuret. He is a Christian knight, but he has gone to the Holy Land, and he has taken service with the Kalif of Baghdad and is killed, leaving behind a queen great with child. Parsifal is born, and he inherits the character of his father.

He is a wonderful youth. When he's about fifteen years old, he is out in the fields. He throws the javelin, kills a bird, and then he is amazed at what he has done, and is sorrowful for killing the bird.

Just then a knight rides past. This is the first knight Parsifal has ever seen! Pretty soon he sees three more knights come by, and they say, "Did you see a knight go by here?" Parsifal gets down on his knees because he thinks they're angels. His mother's told him about nothing but angels. And he says, "What are you?" and they say, "We're knights." "What are knights?" "We're knights." "How does one become a knight?" "Down the way at Arthur's court." "Where's Arthur's court?" "Just down the way."

The unformed social image

So he goes back to his mother and says, "Mother, I want to be a knight." She faints. He still has this intention, and she dresses him up as a fool in a burlap shirt and pants, the trousers halfway down the legs. This absurdly costumed, beautiful boy gets on the farm horse with his quiver of javelins on his back and jogs down the road. As he's approaching Arthur's court, there comes riding out of the court a knight in red armor with a golden cup in his hand. He rides out into the yard. Parsifal rides into court and he understands what is happening. This knight is a king of great power and importance who challenges Arthur because he feels that Arthur has taken some of his property.

He wants to have a jousting tournament to get back his property, and he goes in and insults the court by taking the golden goblet of Queen Guenevere and splashing the wine in her face, saying, "Anyone who wants to amend this, come meet me in the yard."

Just at that time, Parsifal comes in. He says, "I'm gonna be a knight!" and he rides out to meet this chap in the yard. Well, when this knight sees this lout coming at him on his old horse, he won't insult his lance by even using it properly, but turns it around the wrong way and slugs Parsifal off the horse. The horse and Parsifal are on the ground. Parsifal takes his javelin and sends it right through the visor, into the king's eye. That's not the way to kill a king. So Arthur's court is twice disgraced.

Arthur says, "Somebody go out and see what's going on out there." They send out a young page who sees this lout dragging the knight in the red armor around, while trying to get the armor off. He doesn't know how to get the armor off. The page helps him get the armor off and put it on over his other costume, and now he is the Red Knight! Parsifal is helped up onto the knight's powerful charger. He knows how to start the horse, but not how to stop it. They're off, and he's on his adventure.

Forming the social body

In the medieval imagery, the horse represents the dynamism of nature. The rider represents the control of the horse. Well, this guy is out of control, and the horse pulls up toward evening at a little rural castle where there is an old man named Gurnemanz who has lost three sons in the jousting tournaments. He has a little daughter there. Who pulls up at the door? This wonderful horse with the Red Knight on it. Oh my! So he's received, and when they take the armor off they find

this lout underneath. It's a great shock and disappointment. But old Gurnemanz, he knows a piece of human flesh when he sees it, and he sees this is some boy. He takes him in and teaches him the arts and crafts of knightly conduct. The skill in combat. He has a good candidate there. Among the things he tells him – and this is a crucial point – is that a knight does not ask unnecessary questions. Finally he offers the young man his daughter in marriage. Standard marriage situation. Now, the noble heart. Parsifal thinks, "I should not be given a wife; I must earn a wife."

The formed social body

There is a lovely theme of departure where Parsifal steps away and goes off on his adventure, letting the reins fall slack on his horse's neck. The horse leads him to a castle in a valley. Again he is received, this time without that absurd other costume. When you take the armor off a knight, he's covered with rust. He has to be given a bath and then nice soft garments. The castle that he comes into now is the castle of an orphaned queen, a little girl just his own age, and her name is Konduiramours – the one who leads in love.

That night he is asleep and he wakes up around midnight with someone weeping, kneeling at his bed. He has been told by his mother that you kneel only to God. So when he wakes and finds this queen, this little girl, kneeling at his bed, he says, "You don't kneel to anyone but God. If you want to get into bed here, I'll go sleep over there." She says, "I have a story to tell you. If you'll promise not to wrestle with me, I'll get into bed with you and I'll tell you my story." She does get into bed, and the story she tells is: "There is this knight in this neighboring province who wants my castle, me for his wife, and to add me to his kingdom." Typical medieval affair. "You've seen my castle and you know how high my tower is. You've seen how deep the moat is. I would throw myself from that tower into the moat rather than marry that king, who has sent his army against me with his principal lieutenant."

"Well," says Parsifal, "This is no problem. I'll kill him in the morning." She says, "That would be proper, and very good." So in the morning, the drawbridge goes down; down rides the Red Knight. Pretty soon, the leader of the king's force is on his back and Parsifal has thrown his helmet off and is about to cut his head off when the knight says, "I yield." Parsifal says okay, gives him back his helmet, and says, "You go to Arthur's court and tell them that you're my man." During the next few months, a number of people are coming to Arthur's court saying that Parsifal, this Red Knight, has knocked them down. The court thinks, "My God, we've really lost a number here," and they prepare to go out and find where this chap is.

The mesomorph and fulfillment

When he comes back to the castle after having sent this conquered knight off, his little hostess has put her hair up in the way of a married woman. They are now married. So they go to bed. Wolfram says, "Not many ladies in our time would have appreciated that night." He didn't even touch her. After three nights of this kind, he thinks, "Oh, mother told me . . ." and they interlace arms and legs and say, "Oh, this is what we should have been doing all the time." The point of it is that the marriage is a spiritual one first, and the physical act is the consummation. That is the sacrament of marriage.

They have a little child and there is another one on the way when Parsifal thinks, "I wonder about mother." In fact, she died the day he rode away. But he doesn't know anything about this. Now comes the next point. He is now a successful, famous, achieved knight. Also a married man, with a family to which he is loyal. He leaves them only to see about his mother. There is

loyalty there, too. This is a continuation. Having achieved fulfillment in the secular life, he is ready for the spiritual adventure.

The emergence of the endomorphic quality

Again, he leaves the reins slack on the horse's neck, and he comes
to a pond. In the pond is a boat with two men in it, fishing. One
is the Grail King. Parsifal says, "Is there a place where a chap can
spend the night? It's getting late." The Grail King says, "There's
a castle just around the corner. If you reach it – people go astray
here very easily, but if you can come to that castle, just call out
and they'll let down the bridge and you'll be there. If you find it,
I'll be your host tonight." Of course, it's the Grail Castle, and
when he comes in everybody says, "Ahh, this is the knight who
will lift the siege."

We come to this marvelous scene, which takes many, many
pages – it's an allegorical procession that takes place, allegorical
of the virtues of the Grail. The Grail is brought in, which is a vessel
of stone. Now Wolfram's definition of the Grail. It is a stone
vessel that was brought down from heaven by the neutral angels.
In the war of heaven, where Satan's angels were fighting God's
angels, there were also, according to Wolfram, neutral angels.
These neutral angels brought down the Grail. The way between
the pair of opposites. There is no such thing as a good man; there
is no such thing as a bad man. Goodness and evil are relative; they
are not absolutes. Mystical realization embraces good and evil.
The whole religion of Europe is a religion of polarity. God and
Devil. The mystical realization is transcendent of all pairs of
opposites. You move out of your own middle, not in terms of
what is good or evil, or what is profitable or unprofitable, but out
of your center. This will heal the world. The only way to heal the
Wasteland is this transcendence of all concept systems.

The unformed endomorph and absence of compassion

The procession takes place. The king is brought in. He can neither
stand nor sit nor lie. He is in pain. Parsifal is moved by compassion. This is the key. Compassion. Beyond pairs of opposites: "I
am not defending myself. I am opening to the other." But Parsifal

withholds the question "What ails you, Uncle?" that would have healed the king. It would have been an expression of compassion. Instead Parsifal thinks, "A knight does not ask questions." He thinks of his social reputation. He thinks of the ego image, and he puts himself in front of his compassion. The mission fails. The king, a very gracious host, when it is realized that nothing will happen, presents Parsifal with a sword. The sword, however, is going to fail him in a critical moment.

The one beloved in Parsifal's life is Konduiramours. Gawain is the Ladies' Knight. He's been around. Gawain is about thirty-six or so when he sees a woman seated by her horse on a path that he was following, and he is struck by love. Meanwhile, Arthur's court has arrived. They've been searching for Parsifal. A castle called the Chateau Merveille has been disenchanted by Gawain. It was a castle where five hundred ladies and fifty knights were held under spell separate from each other, and Gawain managed to release them from this. So Gawain is going to be married, and all these knights are here – it's a great big party. Then Parsifal arrives. Parsifal is received and the wedding party is going on, and as Wolfram says, "There was love in the pavilions." It was a lovely, wonderful thing. Parsifal thinks, "With all this going on here, I have in my mind only my wife, Konduira-mours. I can't stand this. I am going to leave." So he rides away out of loyalty to his wife.

Disorganizing the mesomorph and initiating the endomorph

As he's riding away, there comes out of the forest before him a pagan knight. The two ride at each other. They unhorse each other. They go at each other with their swords, and Parsifal's sword breaks on the knight's helmet, and the pagan knight, when he sees his opponent without a weapon, throws his own weapon away and says, "I don't fight a man without a weapon."

The two of them sit down and they take their helmets off, and the other knight is black and white. It's Parsifal's brother. There is a beautiful scene of recognizing that the pair of opposites are really one.

Then Parsifal says, "There's a great party down the road. Perhaps you would enjoy it." So the two go back to the party and Wolfram says – the other knight's name is Feirfiz – he was greatly appreciated by the ladies, perhaps because of his interesting complexion. While they are there, the Grail messenger comes and tells Parsifal, "You can come back to the Grail Castle." No one has ever come to the Grail Castle twice. It has to be done once. But because of his loyalty, he can come back. Because of the other knight's noble heart, throwing his sword away, he can come too. So we have a pagan and a Christian going to the Grail Castle to see what has happened. The point is the noble heart, not your religious profession.

The fully formed endomorph

We go back to the Grail Castle; the king is healed; but then it is realized when this beautiful girl comes in carrying the Grail that this pagan knight, this Muslim, can't see the Grail. All he can see are the beautiful eyes of this girl. The people talk around a bit and decide that the problem is that he hasn't been baptized. In comes an old priest with a baptismal font that is empty. He tips the font toward the Grail, and it fills with water. The name of the Grail is Lapis Excilis, one of the names for the philosopher's stone, which represents the same thing the Grail represents: the final union of pairs of opposites in the high transcendent spiritual realization. That is what compassion is, too. The union of a pair of opposites. "I am thou" is one passion between us. Compassion. *Mitleid.* The baptismal font is filled with alchemical water. Feirfiz is to be baptized. No sooner is he baptized than an inscription appears on the Grail.

The king now is healed, Parsifal becomes the Grail King,

he is reunited with Konduiramours & the family,

and they all lived

happily ever

after.

PABLO PICASSO, "MEDIANT À LA BEQUILLE," 1904

CHAPTER 7

Compassion, Transformation, and Rebirth

Keleman: Parsifal is a story about how we use ourselves and grow in the face of our life challenges. Parsifal's quest is to find a way to grow his compassion and empathy. With these new qualities, he makes a relationship to the king, opening to the transcendent.

Campbell: The reason I think it's worth talking about the myth of Parsifal is this idea of compassion as the highest spiritual realization. Compassion means "suffering with." How can anyone so experience the pain and danger of another, forgetting his own self-protection? He moves spontaneously to the other's rescue, even at the loss of his own life. That is compassion.

That is the recognition of a metaphysical truth. You and the other are one. You are of the one life in two aspects. This is going past pairs of opposites; that art thou. Going past pairs of opposites – good and evil – is the key to the refreshment of the Wasteland.

When you hold to the idea of "I will serve, and I will not submit," rather than yielding to compassion, then you hold honor against love. That's the Wasteland.

When you are in service to a phenomenon, to a human being, to a chorus, to a dog, or anything, it means putting yourself in play. It's that compassion which is the essence of the Grail experience. Parsifal, after his failure – this is one of the big points – realized what a mistake he had made in not expressing his compassion. He gave himself up for five years to getting back to that castle. He had been told by a hermit that you don't go back to the Grail Castle. This has to be done on the first visit, without intention. He said, "I'm going back." He was brought back after his expression of loyalty to Konduiramours, when he left that great party and met his brother and they had that fight. There his quality of the noble heart was made known, and the Grail messenger came and brought him back. When the hermit who told him that he couldn't go back learned of this, he said, "By your courage and your service to this court, you have changed the laws of God."

Out of man come the laws of life. They are not put on you. We're taught the laws that are put on us from outside. But the divine power is really within. When we open to it, we open to compassion. The German word tells you a little more clearly than the English – *Mitleid* – "suffering with." Compassion. You've gone past separateness. This quest for the Grail is the quest for that level within yourself which is beyond the little boundary of your ego thoughts. You break through to the human. Anything can break you through to that. The moment of compassion is the most effective.

In service to a larger force

I am reminded of that saying of D. H. Lawrence's about how fearful an experience it is to not be in the hands of a bigger force. Of course, that's what *Parsifal* is about. Not that one shouldn't serve – but serve what? We are part of a living process that is bigger than our little personality. What's our relationship to that? Is it the same relationship that we had toward our mothers and fathers? Or is it different? Parsifal discovers that the way he related to his mother and absent father is not the way that one should relate to a bigger force that drives one's life. Step outside the societal bounds and you have to take on a bigger view, experience.

It is my own personal belief that whatever we want in the larger sense is available to us in ordinary existence. That's part and parcel of how I understand the odyssey of Parsifal. In the ordinary life also resides that other level of meaning. In the pursuit of learning how to be a warrior so that you can ward off the invaders, you also learn of your own somatic unconscious.

Transformation

In this context, the serpent for me is an interesting animal. Not because it sheds its skin, but because when it moves, it is continually changing shape. And with each undulation, its body image shifts. This constantly shifting body image is its somatic psychic organ. A snake is an animal with a thousand shapes, yet a snake. You have the same configuration with the three tissue layers. They express energy, action, information. They represent surface, middle layer, and inside – endo, meso, ecto. They retain their shape while they are involved in changing shape. We experience and perceive at the same time the persistence of the snake and its changing shape. Both messages are part of our somatic consciousness.

The voice of compassion

The integrity of our somatic process is like the snake. A moving shape. In human relationships, the experiencing-self part of our somatic process must trust in its own continually changing shape. Parsifal didn't trust his visceral responses; he was proceeding by social rules. He had to learn to have heart, to be empathetic, to identify with the king's illness.

Do you trust your process? Not your lust, but your process, so that your responses speak and your body's mind supports them rather than the social orders that you were given. Do you voice your compassion, or do you remember that knights don't ask questions? That is the test that Parsifal fails: the emergence of his emotional nature. Parsifal intuits that he responded differently from what he felt inside. Then he becomes faithful to his body's inner process.

This awareness of his somatic process helps him on his way to his adult humanity. One of the things is that Parsifal is in danger of forgetting his uncle's plight, his genetic heritage. He neglects the adult future. He doesn't have compassion for the wounded other.

Using himself differently

How can you use yourself bodily to enact what you are perceiving, or what you were taught to enact? How does the body self disorganize and reorganize emotional attitudes so that it can act in accordance with its own somatic ability, which is its destiny. That's what comes out in Parsifal.

To use yourself differently is the key to your salvation. Never mind changing the old man, the Grail King, who lacks the fulfillment necessary for his position. No, the answer remains with Parsifal. The old man is affected by how Parsifal uses himself.

Changing the world or reorganizing ourselves

We should make a distinction between revolutionizing the world and reorganizing ourselves. To the degree that psychological insight has been used for political purposes, it's another manipulation of the person. Salvation in the sense of initiation is lost. Salvation becomes a crusade to change the political and social structure. Then we don't have any insight into the individual's somatic psyche, but we want to change the collective bodily psyche. In both situations, you need somatic experience – not just insight into the role that you're playing, but the feel of the somatic organization that accompanies that role – so that you can change the way that you relate to yourself.

How do you use yourself?

In my practice of formative psychology, my advice is to learn the organization of your own process and reorganize yourself. How are you somatically alive in the world? Don't take on the image of others. Worry about how you use yourself.

From your insides

In one respect, Parsifal's conflict is that he starts out as a mother's boy, a man who takes his orders from society. As a man who has never had a father, he looks to the outside to give him a sense of maleness. When he meets the king, he realizes, "Oh my God, I missed the boat by not saying, 'What ails you, Uncle?' " So then he has to work from his inside. And it says very clearly, because he was sincere of heart, he went back to his own self to see what he had missed. Since he worked on becoming an adult from inside, from his own bodily process, he becomes the Grail.

The Grail is your given life

The hero's journey is about trying to live out your own destiny, and not the one society defines – the smart student, the successful businessman, the professional lawyer or doctor. This journey means to enter on the path of your own given life and to develop it and overcome from the inside the challenges that it poses. You live from your own body type.

Layers of functions and qualities

Life is a series of shapes. There is Parsifal the boy with his mother, a young man who searches for a father, his growing maturity as he incorporates the lessons from his encounters. In time he enters the world as an adult family man, part of society. All the different shapes of his life, his destiny, are lived. He forms his evolution, from unformed boy to mature adult.

Parsifal integrates these various functions. His quest reveals how he brings together different qualities, such as assertiveness and tenderness, the fighting man and the compassionate man. He blends tenderness, understanding and empathy, with action to form an individual and a more adult somatic entity.

This integration opens the door to the nature of self-organization. I am not interested in the resolution of opposites, but in the ability of opposites to organize a somatic form. Opposites are the tensions that are part of the formative process. When we can embody these tensions, we form our individuality. We all are foolish and wise, wild and tame.

When you restrict yourself to a single identity, you make yourself either too rigid or too formless. We need to understand the creative tension among endo, ecto, and meso, the creative tension that holds the person together. These types are not competitive or conflicting, but move in a repelling and attracting pulse. If you understand that rhythm in yourself, you understand the rhythm of your own organization and your own true identity. Potency means being able to be true to what is your form, to be transparent to that which is transcendent. The shape of yourself reveals what animates you.

Truth vs. hearsay

Parsifal didn't understand the nature of being an adult. He took it from hearsay and the code of the knights. He violated his inherited endomorphic reality.

To be twice born

The *Parsifal* myth teaches us that experience stimulates deep bodily truths, truths that urge us to form a personal self. When you know this, you begin a new life, enter a new world. Like Parsifal, you can take on new roles. At the turn of the century, William James said that there are the once born and the twice born. The once born are very nice but very uninteresting people. It is the twice born who really understand something and who reconstruct themselves from the ground floor up at some major point. Our society gives all of us the chance to be twice born. To be twice born is to form again our bodied self from our ancestral body.

Myth and biology are our source of reference

The *Parsifal* myth is a tale of formation in its own time. It is a story about the forming of all of the attributes that make us human: our bodily consciousness, our inwardness, own divinity. *Parsifal* is in fact a statement about a biological epistemology, a biological ontology from ancient times to our own modern times about how myth and biology are a source of reference.

Parsifal is the bringing of compassion and understanding and honor into one's life. There is a biological, emotional truth: to use yourself to generate and express compassion and understanding; to maintain the honor of your own process and recognize it in another. In this sense, embryology is cosmology and the somatic process is an evolutionary drama, our personal cosmology.

CHAPTER 8

Our Life Stories

AMONG THE STORIES embedded in our cellular self are these:

THE MESOMORPH: I am born for heroic adventures; to live, to hunt, to replicate, to act.

THE ENDOMORPH: I live to seek what fills me and satisfies me; to incorporate, make part of me.

THE ECTOMORPH: I am born to migrate, to go from place to place, to be alone. I am born to be with, not part of.

STANLEY KELEMAN

There is a wonderful paper by Schopenhauer called "An Apparent Intention in the Fate of the Individual." He says that when you get to be a certain age – let's say over sixty – and look back over your life, there is a plot that you recognize.

Who wrote it? There is a continuity, a plot, a wonderful plot. He said it's a little bit like reading a certain kind of novel. In the English language it would be Dickens, where it rambles along and then you realize, "Oh, this character that just seemed to be in my life by chance was a fundamental structuring factor in the building of my life." What seemed to be accidental actually got built into a plot. Who wrote it?

At the same time, you've got to realize that you've played roles like that in other people's lives. These people that influenced you, you influenced them. There is a kind of great symphony. James Joyce comes up with this idea, which underlies his great novel, Finnegan's Wake. All of these different lives are influencing each other to illuminate, to unfold them; to get them to unfold and find out who and what they are.

Schopenhauer asks another question: "Can anything happen to you that doesn't fit into the plot or that didn't fit in the plot?" It looked like damage when it came, but it built a story. And the story didn't go where you wanted it to go, perhaps. But nonetheless, you were writing that story. Could there be a writer who was coordinating all these stories? He comes up with this lovely image at the end. He says, "The world is like a dream dreamed by a single dreamer in which all the dream characters are dreaming, too. They are dreaming their lives, and the whole thing coordinates in a kind of mysterious harmony." Looking back and thinking of my own life in terms of what Schopenhauer said, there's a well-structured plot that wasn't the one I intended at all, even though I thought it was intended.

You may think you are doing it from up here, in the cortex, but something in the brain is really what's building your plot. When you look back with this idea that Schopenhauer gives, just think of your life as, "It is an organized story. Who is the author?" If you don't see the organization, look harder. You'll see it. It's a consistently structured story.

Joseph Campbell

You carry the story

Whether you know it or not, you are also writing a novel of yourself. You carry around a story inside you. So you can ask, "What story am I living out? How am I going to go about perceiving it?" Our biological story is to be born, to grow, to replicate, and to die. All societies form an organization that tries to perpetuate themselves and their group identity. It is God's commandment to be fruitful and multiply. You give the tribe a future if you obey the rules that the ancestors followed in organizing their form of existence.

All stories also have an emotional reality. This emotional reality is the character that we play. All of us play a social character and a personal character, and we play it out on the stage of our social interactions. They become part of our organizing process, which helps to form our life; we practice these roles daily.

Your body posture is a story. The story itself is also an experience. Discovering how we invoke our different emotional shapes helps us to discover the stories that we live. When we pay attention to our stories, we know something about how we body our life. That is one of the functions of mythology.

Participate in your story

All inanimate existence is a cycle of forming and unforming. We all live this formative process, and it manifests itself in the stories we tell and in how we experience being alive and changing shape, from young to old. That's the premise of my work – to bring to the foreground the way you can participate in your own shaping and unshaping.

From primordial soup to particular end

The early evolutionists may have wanted to deny that there was a creation; therefore, they have the primordial soup that accidentally brewed animate forms. But the story of evolution is still the story of our origins. And it still tells how we came from an undifferentiated and great ocean into existence as a particular form in the pool of life, moving through certain stations toward a particular end.

Storytelling

Storytelling is a form of integration and a script for bodying. It might be called the somatic imagination. William Blake, in his wonderful mythological sagas, spoke of the transformation of bodies. One born from another and back again. Blake's *Four Zoas* was a myth of bodies making and changing shape.

Whether we like it or not, we are incarnated. We are bodies on this planet, and all myth and all stories seek the origin and the end of our somatic structure. Myth as story is the life of our body in one or another of its forms. We are all making up stories, finding stories, finding facts to talk about our somatic origin, its growth, and its end.

The body's shape is part of a continuity

The body is important because it is our continuity. It is our link to the past and give validity to our present shape. In telling your story, look for the somatic shapes. This is the way to experience our origins.

Our need to know our somatic origins becomes even more crucial as our connection to nature decreases, as the abstractions in the educational realm and in the media escalate. Paying attention to our personal and family stories is like entering a forest. It teaches us to understand our personal somatic origin and the origin that we all share and seek. Whom does the Grail serve? It serves life's bodies.

REMBRANDT, SELF-PORTRAIT, 1652
Kunsthistorisches Museum, Vienna

PART FOUR

Initiation:
Deepening Our
Somatic Humanity

Somatic humanity is a recognized similarity
of responses between ourselves and others.

CHAPTER 9

Deepening Your Fate

I REMEMBER an interview that Dick Cavett had with Jorge Luis Borges, the South American writer. At that time, Borges was going blind and he was saying how his world was now in shades of blue and gray. That was his world. Everything was indistinguishable except for those hues. Then Borges made a remarkable statement. He said, "My father had the same disease as his father, and so I feel that I am living the destiny of my ancestors, telling stories about the dark." He was forming his life as a writer without external sight.

Borges was an ectomorphic man living as a mesomorphic writer and storyteller. He accepted his biological fate and continued to act as a blind story maker. He accepted his fate as a blind man in action.

We take our sight for granted, without connection to our ancestors. We've moved far away from blood connection as reference and destiny. But to become a mature person, the person you were meant to be, is to know who you are: to know your fate – as an ecotomorph, endomorph, or mesomorph. Your task is to know the divine mystery of reproduction, communication, the mystery of death and transformation. To taste that is to deepen your life experience.

STANLEY KELEMAN

There is a word that we have in English, and we have forgotten the meaning of that word. The word is "weird." Shakespeare, in Macbeth, has the three weird sisters. That word "weird" means these are the Three Fates. The Moslems think of kismet – fate – as something that is put upon them by God. The word "weird" is related to the German word "Werden" – becoming. Your weird, your fate, comes right out of yourself. This is not something that is put upon you. Your face is your fortune, you might say. What you have as a body and as potentialities and whatever is your weird.

Nietzsche has this wonderful thing of AMOR FATI – loving your fate. "The Fates lead those who will. Those who won't, they drag."

Joseph Campbell

◯◯

Keleman: Telling a story acts as an organizer to help you to body your experience. Not only does it help you to organize meaning, but meaning is grown from your body self. The storytelling organizes your responses into a narrative form that you can use to give meaning and direction to experience.

Campbell: One of the most noble dragon-killing stories I know is in the old Anglo-Saxon poem *Beowulf*. Beowulf became the chief of the great people, and in his old age there came a dragon who began to harass the whole neighborhood. They asked the chief how to kill that dragon.

Old Beowulf was now very old, and he knew that he was not going to survive the dragon fight. He was going to kill the dragon, but he would be killed too; he had a premonition of this. There is one line that came out, and when I read it, it was like fire. He was sitting and just thinking it over before going to face this monster. "Weird was very near." The fulfillment of his life destiny was what he was about to face.

Keleman: Stories are about how our own somas are created, grow, and disappear. The organism is telling itself stories about growing, about preparing to grow. Beowulf going to meet the dragon is a very beautiful invention about making order for growing up and developing an ego and dealing with the forces that are unknown to him, rather than simply being in life without any preparation.

Campbell: Experience. That's the key word. There is a certain irony in the quest themes that I've noticed, and it's in myths as well. We have this whole vocabulary of looking for the "meaning of life." No one is really looking for the meaning of life. People are looking for an experience of life. The home that you came from was an experience of life.

Keleman: Bodily experience is the key. The experience of your body. Storytelling synthesizes somatic experience. It organizes the elements of experience into a body form that gives us a personal shape, a direction, and even a felt sense of meaning. That's why I insist on looking for the body in a story, rather than looking for symbols and their meanings. In this way we experience the cortical man talking to the subcortical man.

CHAPTER 10

The Return to a
Somatic Reference

TO BE EMBODIED is to participate in a migration from one body form to another. Each of us is a nomad, a wave that has duration for a time and then takes on a new somatic shape. This perpetual transformation is the subject of all myth.

STANLEY KELEMAN

I don't know how many of you have been in one of the Lascaux caves, but it is a terrific experience. They are enormous; some of them are a mile long. Nobody ever lived in those caves. They were temple caves. They were caves for the hunting initiation, the young men who were going to kill the animals. They became men learning not only how to kill the animal, but the ritual that went with it. So again, you have the sanctification, the mythologization, of a life act.

When you go down in those caves, you don't know what direction you are moving in. They are totally dark. The world above seems like a shadow world. Those animals, the beautiful surety of lines with which they were put on the wall. They were done with a line that was like that of Japanese ink on silk. Their line included a rise in the rock, which would be the horse or the animal. Those were the Platonic ideals of the animals that were up there. It was to these that the animal was returned by the ritual. They go down, back into the womb again for rebirth. This is just a shadow game. The Maya game of all our living and our dying, the big things down here. And it is most amazing that those paintings stayed there for thirty thousand years, waiting for us to find them again.

When we were down there, the guide suddenly turned out all the lights. Well, my God. They didn't have electrical lights; they had these flickering torches. That was the best light they could have had. This is the transformation by which all things come, the way in which your psyche shifts center. The world up there is experienced as being a secondary world when you are down in those caves.

And that puts you into something inside you, the enduring thing in you. Because each of us is just a little flicker of an eternal life that is in us. We are functions of an eternal life. There is an inexhaustible energy to store up these forms. And that is what we really are. We get attached to the little local forms. You have to go down to a cave like that to have it shown to you.

So these were mythical as well as hunting initiations. This is a terrific thing. It comes along with the human being, a sense of imaging. They didn't have a model of the animal sitting in front of them like an artist in a studio with a bowl of fruit. They are all in the mind. And those animals are perfect. It is something to see a mammoth and know it was drawn by someone who had seen mammoths. It is very much alive in that cave. It is enough to generate a whole new generation of mammoths. The power of the human being to image is what comes.

Joseph Campbell

Somatic initiation

What a powerful event it is to become a hunter – or a father, or a mother, or a worker – when we are presented with experiences that suggest how to act and are galvanized by our emotional currents. This initiation forces you to act differently, to use yourself differently. It is a new inner structure that is being created, another body reality. When you take a young boy out and you show him the skills of hunting, killing is no longer a random act, but an act that requires self-mastery and recognition of a reality. The transmission of experience is the transmission of somatic image, which organizes another level of the somatic self, of how to act.

Somatic transmission

When we know that the transmission of experience is somatic, we can see how to find our way back to a somatic reference. It brings another body into existence. This mimics creation. From our body's deep desires, tissue consciousness grows. The body communicates it in stories that we call myth.

Primary connection

The soma's process is a primary source of self-referring. It is intercellular movement, movement of cells as an organized colony. This motility is our primary human experience. We are embedded in a palpable living field. It is the biosphere, the protoplasmic ocean around us, between us, in us. As far as I understand, myth comes directly from this process.

Experiential and imagistic reference

Keleman: I remember lying down and being fascinated by a motile internal image that I could feel. From inside my torso came a snake. It entered my brain, going from the right side to the left. I felt visceral movement in my belly and throat. Then an image of a snake moving through me. The body's inner movement experienced itself as motility and also as image. The body's experience and its brain's images are one process with two expressions.

When I realized this, it affirmed my somatic work. That method lets my clients see how the body organizes its mind, and how the body's brain reorganizes the body's experiences. This is the somatic process continually changing; the snake, which I experienced inside me, and also as image.

It was an uncanny experience to have this snake in me and also to have something moving inside me. I call that being in the mythic realm. It was part and parcel of a cellular motility, a stream that was felt and recognized, in my brain and in my body. This is what the people in the Lascaux caves must have experienced.

Campbell: Symbolically, the serpent is the life power bound to the earth. It sheds its skin when the moon does, and so represents something that is deeper and more continuous than a specific life occasion. It sheds its skin, it sheds a personality, it sheds a way of life and turns into another one. And so it becomes symbolic of the power of life in the field of time and space.

The bird, on the other hand, is disengaged from the earth and represents the power of spiritual flight. So these two are in opposition. You have the serpent hypnotizing and then consuming the bird; or you have the bird – a hawk or an eagle – pouncing on the serpent. These are the two images that occur in all kinds of mythology. And then the juncture of the two is the dragon, the flying serpent. These are very strange images. And here we have these two out of the old dinosaur period, the bird and the serpent. The bird's feathers and the serpent's scales are equivalent, and between them comes the mammal, of which the highest, from my point of view, is the human. He finds himself between these two powers.

Keleman: The recognition of the body's pulsatory movement generates images and perceptions that are the alpha and omega of myths. Tissue experience is its foundation. I almost missed that experience by pursuing what the snake "meant" coming out of my bowels and into my head, and what it "meant" going from the right brain to the left. I came up with some fascinating answers. But I almost lost sight of the fact that the body was organizing its own images as a way for the body to talk to itself about itself.

Our images are body experiences. We share this tissue experience. Yet many times we are unaware of it. We need to cultivate it if we want to enter into the human realm. Entering into that realm gives our life a zest that transcends the social philosophy and recognizes the truth of somatic connection.

The body's own process originates myth. The soma organizes its own humanity. This is the process of creation, of the transmission of somatic reality, that the humans of Lascaux bequeathed to us.

Mythic reference is the somatic process

Myth can make what is transparent, what is transcendent, into the somatic process. The body uses its brain to make images of itself and the world. These organized experiences relate us to our own bodies and to others. This is what I call bodily reference and what literature calls mythic thinking.

The metaphors of something moving, something flowing; go with the river, flow with the river – they are talking about an observation in nature – the changing seasons, the moving river – but that would put it on the outside. How about if you felt it in yourself, and then tried to describe how you felt in yourself? Outpouring, the ray of creation, the breaking of the egg, the word – there is light; or even of our changing bodies – urinating, blood beating inside, waves of giving birth or making love.

Keleman: Throughout my life, I have pursued vigorously a somatic reference, a biological, emotional reference. That is, I have attempted to understand what bodily life is through understanding my own body and its responses, and the relationship between the form I take and who I am. I've discovered that the experience of bodily life borders on the sacred.

Campbell: One way to get yourself in accord with the transcendent is to bring this thing that the mind has thought of as being proper into accord with what is really there. The world as is. To see and affirm the world as is, so that this transcendent energy, this transcendent mystery, is manifest through us, and then we become transparent to the transcendent.

What a bridge! Now when I caught the real majesty of that thought and then was thinking about mythology, I realized that mythology is an instrument for helping you to experience the transcendent. To turn the aspects of your own life, aspects of the world, into a transparency to the transcendent. The deities in all the images of myth point to the transcendent. It neither is nor is not; it's not one, it's not many. One of the problems with most of our schools of theology is that you stop with the god. The god stops you there; he doesn't become transcendent or transparent.

Keleman: Through bodily life you discover we are part of something bigger than ourselves, something that is continuous, even though we ourselves are discontinuous.

CHAPTER 11

Forming Your Somatic Humanity: The Bodying Practice

MYTH is the voice of the body becoming human.

THE GOAL OF SOMATIC WORK is to discern how you experience your embodiment and how you influence your bodily life; to learn how to live with your somatic constitution and how the body captures, preserves, and forms its responses.

Joseph Campbell spoke a great deal about knighthood in the myth of *Parsifal*. To be a knight took training and discipline. The knight had to learn about upright posture, how to move and make gestures that conveyed aristocratic background, both gentlemanly and warlike.

This somatic learning is important to all human development. But it is not a question of training. It is a question of purposefully influencing your somatic development. This is the basis of the somatic method.

In the *Masks of God* series, Campbell made the point that we could read back the story of creation by looking at the myths mankind has structured to articulate its experience. The mythic hero has a thousand faces: this hero is an expression of creation continually rebodying itself. How we have come to be and how we can be embodied are the themes of both ancient and modern myth. Being embodied is a statement that we are here; it defines a physical relationship with ourselves, with the world, and with what we call the transcendent.

Human embodiment is a continuous process. The person who is volitionally engaged in this process is the protagonist of our modern myth. As formative beings, we need a method of working with our own bodying process. This method must address the fact that the struggle to rebody our experiences and our emotional expressions takes work. This method of working allows each of us to begin to influence our somatic shape.

The Bodying Practice restores a sense of our somatic sanity. It restores the feeling of being a somatic entity and the sense of being embodied. It provides a sense of inwardness, an instinctual sense of the natural animal that is part of the reality of our personal and social selves. Not ideals, but the basic responses of the body itself become the reference for what is authentic.

The Bodying Practice facilitates self-contact. Through this self-contact, we come to learn how we embody ourselves. We learn how we are embodied, how we take part in forming our gestures and expressions of feelings; how we pose emotionally – being proud, being brave. The Bodying Practice invites us to engage in a somatic-emotional dialogue with ourselves to body our experience – that is, to make it ours.

The Bodying Practice works by slowing down the urge to act. When the urge to act is slowed down, a somatic image is formed. It is a snapshot in time of the body's shape. This lets us feel the forms, feelings, and images that accompany our acts. Each bodied state is a part of a sequence. When we freeze or slow down or intensify a somatic moment through the Bodying Practice, past emotional shapes appear. The Bodying Practice makes these past shapes distinct from present ones and helps us to experience the continuity of our body expression.

Through the Bodying Practice we stabilize a somatic expression so we can recognize the warrior's stance or the mothering pose. In this way we can receive the shape's intensity and give it a distinct identity.

The Bodying Practice consists of five steps.

STEP ONE *Observe.*

In this step we identify and recognize the body in its present behavior pattern. It is something felt; it stands out. "My neck is stiff."

STEP TWO *Exaggerate.*

In this step we use our volition to intensify the behavior pattern that we have identified. If we experience pride as a stiff neck, we stiffen the neck more. This makes the stiffness pattern come into its full form. When we are enacting "pride," or "stiffen the neck," we are using our brain – which is making maps of body attitudes and linking words to past behavior – and reinforcing past behavior in the present. Step two makes vivid how we can influence this behavior volitionally, which gives us the opportunity to stiffen less – that is, to be less prideful.

STEP THREE *Deintensify.*

If we have volitionally intensified a behavior pattern – in this case, a contraction – then we can also disassemble that pattern. That is, we can make it more intense and then undo it. As we do this, we expand our influence into the reflex world, into the nonvolitional world, because the dialogue between "do it more" and "do it less" begins to be extended deeper, from cortex to brain stem via the midbrain. We are able to touch the action and able to delay it.

STEP FOUR *Wait.*

After we have disassembled some of the behavior pattern, we find ourselves in what I call the waiting place, a pause. We contain what we have just disassembled, so that there is no dispersal. This pause state is where feelings and images, past motor behavior, memories, and past experiences of excitement come up; as in dreams, these are rehearsals for our future bodying behavior.

STEP FIVE *Reorganize.*

In this step we participate volitionally in what is being reassembled. The body's brain begins to support and direct muscle activity, to practice, try out, repeat an action. The brain is personalizing the body's new efforts. Step five is practice at performing.

THESE FIVE STEPS are the rules for disorganizing and reorganizing form. This is formative psychology. The goal of formative psychology is to get us to feel our situation so that we can find a way to form our experiences and to be intimate with our life. This is the key to creativity and satisfaction. When our experiences are bodied, they give rise to emotional values such as cooperation, tradition, altruism, love. These values then find an expression that differentiates our inherited emotional acts, forming a personal bodied consciousness.

To see ourselves as a psychological self gives rise to a nonbodied existence. It encourages fragmentation, the dissociation of the mental from its source. It blinds us to our temporality, to the reality of our birth and death. All this happens when we develop the mind at the expense of the soma.

Working with the *Bodying Practice*, we can begin to experience our body structure. The practice lets our body speak, lets it find its inner voice. As we learn to be intimate with what wants to form, we use myths to help organize or orient our experience.

The *Bodying Practice* is linked to the bodying process. Bringing the body close to its protoplasmic or mythic state, the *Bodying Practice* helps the body to become intimate with its own generative functions. The story that grows out of this process is our own personal creation myth.

Parsifal:
Transformation from Pride to Compassion

THE DEATH OF THE IMAGE of knighthood brings about Parsifal's deeper authentic image, which is compassion. He is then able to recognize the suffering of the king, and to use his compassion to heal him.

This exercise follows the growth of Parsifal, from pride to compassion, which instructs our reality and humanity. Compassion depends on our ability to be present with ourselves. By deepening that ability, this exercise begins the deepening of compassion.

STEP ONE

Make the posture of pride.

Notice the chest. Notice the back of the neck, mouth, throat and eyes. Are you looking down your nose? What feeling accompanies this?

STEP TWO

Dramatize what you've just recognized.

Do it more strongly. Give the muscles more tone. More intensity. This may stiffen the chest more, or fix the eyes. What kind of experience is this? What feelings or images surface?

STEP THREE

To undramatize, to end the dramatization of intensified pride: slightly undo, allow some of the pattern to come apart (not relax). This should be done in at least three steps. This gives distinct layers to pride.

STEP FOUR

When you undo, there is generally a pause where images and feelings are like a dream state, are being reshuffled, recollected, brought together into a vision, insight, or sense of direction. This is collecting the body's response into a greater sense of compassion.

STEP FIVE

This is like waking up.

We begin to practice, body, what we have begun to realize in step four. It is a deepening. It is making layers in. It is deepening our embodiment and therefore, our compassion.

୧୭

Myth in Daily Life

JULY IS HOT, and this July is no different. Awakening this vacation morning to a glorious brightness, I realize that I have spent a fitful night. The aching in my brain, the muscular cramping of my head, neck, shoulders, and chest, tell me that I am still in the warrior's posture of teacher-therapist. I have not totally left my recent workshop, although I am fifty miles away, at the edge of the sea. I am still enacting the drama, straining to pay attention, to be present. Finally, I begin to disengage, to undo the upper body's stance and emotional configuration that is splitting me into two states: to be responsive to others and to be responsive to myself.

The drama

As I intensify my pattern of somatic presence, I dramatize the stiffening and experience the chest-up of body and attention that is part of all intense human engagement. I feel my identity with Parsifal. I, too, struggle to respond to my own pulse.

The inner somatic ocean

This July morning, I changed the mesomorphic healer in me to settle down into my endomorphic, visceral pulses. In undoing the attitudes that were separating me from my endomorphic self, my Grail Castle emerged.

A visceral warmth filled me as I stood on the deck of the high-ceilinged wood house, looking at a primeval habitat, a lagoon. There was silence on this protected inlet of sea. Egrets and other birds stood stark still. Sleek black heads of seals broke the water's surface. I felt the pulse of my belly and a warm tide swelling into my chest and head. I was resonating to my own somatic sea. I was magnetized and drawn from what was in me to what was out there. I was standing in a silence where all things shimmered, like the pulse coming from my belly and chest. As I strode through the house where my family slept, the silence still prevailed.

Getting on my bike, I cycled around the lagoon, leaving behind the civilized world of the rented vacation house, leaving my family behind. I pedaled around the tar road to the bend in the path, past civilization's edge. In my receptive mood and posture, my boundaries were porous: water, fog, clouds, sky, white and black birds, shadows in the sky and in the water's mirror – all formed a flux of membranes, of embedded shapes.

The return

I experienced where I begin and the world ends. I am embedded in the world and in myself; the world is in me, and I in it. Vivid forms are conjured by the vapors of dawn; they are connected to me, in me. I am simultaneously flux and form, concrete and immaterial, a pulse of here and there, timeless and timed. I am the ferryman, Parsifal, the waiting king, the ancient and young Stanley.

I bicycled along the path alongside the lagoon, a participant in a day that could otherwise have been ordinary; I cycled toward the sea, facing the endless horizon. In the evening tide, I detected the fragile currents, furtively seeping back from the neck of the inlet, as the ocean calls the lagoon home. The egrets stood stark still on long legs on the mud bottom, their slender necks and pointed beaks leading their black eyes toward the sea's edge. They were waiting, with some knowing, for the return of the tide on which their life depends.

The appearance of the Grail

I EXPERIENCE a basic body truth, a timeless eternal drama of somatic appearance and disappearance. My body and its mind are layered, are part of the circle of existence, a pulse within a bigger pulse.

I AM EXPERIENCING

the endomorph, mesomorph, and ectomorph

of my body's layers on the Lagoon, bicycling from eternity toward

my future, part of an endless chain of changing human forms.

I see that this somatic reality

is my myth.

෨෧

REMBRANDT
A VIEW OF THE AMSTEL WITH A MAN BATHING, c. 1654–55
Kupferstichkabinett, Staatliche Museum, Berlin-Dahlem

STANLEY KELEMAN,
born in Brooklyn, New York, in 1931, is director of the Center for Energetic Studies in Berkeley, California. He has been practicing and developing somatic therapy for over thirty-five years, and is a pioneer in his study of the life of the body and its connection to the sexual, emotional, and imaginative aspects of human experience. Through his writings and continuing practice, Keleman has developed a methodology and conceptual framework for the life of the body which are to be found in his recent books, *Emotional Anatomy* and *Embodying Experience.*

JOSEPH CAMPBELL,
educator, author, and editor, was educated at Columbia University, University of Paris, and the University of Munich. For nearly forty years, he taught at Sarah Lawrence College where he was a member of the literature faculty. He is author of the four-volume study of world mythologies collectively titled *The Masks of God;* also *The Hero with a Thousand Faces,* and *The Flight of the Wild Gander,* and editor of *The Portable Jung* and *The Portable Arabian Nights.* He appeared with Bill Moyers on a television series, *The Power of Myth,* which was aired following his death in 1987. Director George Lucas credits *The Hero with a Thousand Faces* as the template and inspiration for the *Star Wars* films.